The Priest's Communion with Christ
Dispelling Functionalism

By Father Eugene M. Florea

The Institute for Priestly Formation
IPF Publications

NIHIL OBSTAT: Father Matthew J. Gutowski, JCL

IMPRIMATUR: Most Reverend George J. Lucas
                Archbishop of Omaha, Nebraska
                May 4, 2018

THE INSTITUTE FOR PRIESTLY FORMATION
IPF Publications
2500 California Plaza
Omaha, Nebraska 68178-0415
www.IPFPublications.com

Printed in the United States of America
ISBN-13: 978-0-9981164-2-6

Cover design by Timothy D. Boatright
Vistra Communications
Tampa, Florida

THE INSTITUTE FOR PRIESTLY FORMATION
Mission Statement

The Institute for Priestly Formation was founded to assist bishops in the spiritual formation of diocesan seminarians and priests in the Roman Catholic Church. The Institute responds to the need to foster spiritual formation as the integrating and governing principle of all aspects for priestly formation. Inspired by the biblical-evangelical spirituality of Ignatius Loyola, this spiritual formation has as its goal the cultivation of a deep interior communion with Christ; from such communion, the priest shares in Christ's own pastoral charity. In carrying out its mission, the Institute directly serves diocesan seminarians and priests as well as those who are responsible for diocesan priestly formation.

THE INSTITUTE FOR PRIESTLY FORMATION
Creighton University
2500 California Plaza
Omaha, Nebraska 68178-0415
www.priestlyformation.org
ipf@creighton.edu

TABLE OF CONTENTS

FOREWORD

In the Gospel of John, Jesus proclaims, "I am the light of the world. Whoever follows me will not walk in darkness, but will have the light of life" (Jn 8:12). This teaching of Jesus is of particular importance for priests to ponder because Jesus will also say, "You are the light of the world. A city set on a mountain cannot be hidden" (Mt 5:14).

While the command to be "the light of the world" is a challenge that Jesus extends to everyone who chooses to follow Him, for priests who minister *in persona Christi*, it has a more profound meaning. How do we who have been called to exercise the charism of priestly ministry in the Church live out our vocations in a manner that has been enlightened by Christ and brings light to those who live in darkness?

However we understand the many forms of darkness that can afflict the human condition, the priestly identity cannot be hidden or, more commonly, lost through the distraction of identifying what it means to be a priest with the tasks or functions that priests are called to fulfill every day.

While I have often been inspired and blessed by the sacrificial efforts of priests who work long and hard to minister to the faithful, I ask myself, "What do the faithful need most from us?" Without question, they need the grace of the Sacraments. They need the hope that is found in Sacred Scripture when they hear of God's saving activity though time. They need to feel welcomed into a community of faith where—through prayer, works of charity, and fraternal support—they have come to experience a strong sense of belonging; but from their priests, more than anything else, they need to see an image of Christ.

Every Christian is called to "put on the Lord Jesus Christ" (Rm 13:14). Priests are called to an even higher standard because we are to conform ourselves to Christ in a manner by which we will be the light of Christ within the community we serve in a unique way that is rooted in the grace of priestly ordination.

All the good works that we do in the name of Christ, all the sacrifices that a priest will make, all the words of wisdom that a priest will preach, all the Sacraments that a priest will celebrate, all of this and much more means little if a priest has not conformed himself to Christ in a manner that through him, the light of Christ is like, "A city set on a mountain [that] cannot be hidden."

In *The Priest's Communion with Christ: Dispelling Functionalism*, Fr. Eugene Florea provides a message of encouragement. Reflecting on the chapters of this book will provide a challenge, but more importantly, it will light a path for priestly ministry that will free priests from the dangers of functionalism, freeing us to root our lives in the One who is both the "light of the world" and the rock upon which all priestly ministry rests.

Most Reverend Thomas J. Olmsted
Bishop of Phoenix

INTRODUCTION

Over the last several years, I have had the great privilege of participating in and assisting with many of the programs of The Institute for Priestly Formation (IPF). It is this experience with IPF, as well as my ministry as the director of a house of prayer for priests in the diocese of Phoenix that led me to want to explore the topic of communion with Christ as the antidote to functionalism in the priesthood. Through this ministry to priests, I have come to see, over and over again, that the happiness and sense of fulfillment for which we priests long is found only by entering into deep, intimate communion with the Blessed Trinity.

Many diocesan priests today feel overworked, underappreciated, and lonely. This leads to a sense of meaninglessness, which may even be accompanied by a temptation to leave the priestly ministry altogether. The problem is a crisis in priestly identity that is rooted in a functional approach to priesthood, wherein the emphasis lies on "doing" rather than on "being." This "functionalism," as it pertains to the priesthood, describes an approach to life in which a priest derives his identity from his activity, his work, his success, his titles, his rewards, his achievements, his fidelity to his duties, and other such externally based things.

The antidote to functionalism is for the priest to place "communion with Christ" at the very center of his existence. The priest discovers his true identity only through his communion with Christ. When the priest is properly grounded in his identity, he will have a clearer sense of mission and, thus, a more fruitful ministry.

In looking at the topic of communion with Christ as an antidote to the problem of functionalism in the contemporary diocesan priesthood, I will explore certain key magisterial and theological texts, beginning in the period immediately prior to the Second Vatican Council, up until the present day. In particular, I will look at Blessed Columba Marmion, whose writings on prayer help to define the phrase "communion with Christ." Next, I will look at the documents from the Second Vatican Council pertaining to the priesthood, with a particular view toward what that Council teaches about how communion with Christ flows from the sacramental character received at priestly ordination. I will then look at what St. John Paul II and Pope Benedict XVI contribute to this discussion. Finally, I will propose that Saint John Mary Vianney, patron saint of priests, is a living image of what communion with Christ "looks like"—that is, that the Curé of Ars is one who lived communion with Christ in a profound way in the midst of his very active parish ministry.

This book is simply a synthesis and presentation of the incredible treasure trove of wisdom that is found in the Church's living tradition on the subject of communion with Christ. I recommend not only reading, but slowly praying with and meditating upon the many substantial quotations from the Church's saints and theologians that are offered as a way of deepening the reader's own communion with the Trinity.

I am deeply grateful to all who made this book possible. First, I am grateful to my Bishop, the Most Reverend Thomas J. Olmsted, who has been continuously supportive. I express my thanks to the faculty and staff of Mundelein Seminary and of The Institute for Priestly Formation for all they have taught me. In particular, I am very grateful to Deacon James Keating, who guided my work every step of the way and offered much wisdom and encouragement. My heartfelt thanks go to Fr. James Rafferty, who provided the initial seed of an idea for this book. I am very grateful to Michelle Funke for editing and preparing this text for publication. I am also deeply grateful to Fr. Michael Fuller, Fr. Scott Harter, Fr. Richard Gabuzda, Fr. John Horn, S.J., Msgr. John Esseff, Miss Kathy Kanavy, as well as the presbyterate and permanent diaconate community of the Diocese of Phoenix who provided many valuable suggestions along the way.

Communion with Christ as the Antidote to Functionalism

A Vignette of Functionalism: Father Ron[1]

Wednesday morning. 6 a.m. The alarm clock goes off. Father Ron wakes up with a feeling of dread. He has a big day ahead of him, and he is not looking forward to it. He wishes it were already Thursday, his day off. He has to give a big talk tonight at the downtown convention center for a national gathering of Catholic youth ministers on the subject of evangelization. Why did he say, "Yes"? He already has so much to do. He was hooked into it by the conference organizers who extolled Fr. Ron's speaking gifts. It is true that he is a gifted speaker and is also very good with the youth, but now he feels the pressure of needing to "perform." It feels like the more stellar his homilies and other speaking engagements are, the more the pressure builds to deliver even more the next time. But he feels like he has run out of steam. His creativity is slowing down. He has not prepared anything for the talk yet.

But that conference is not until tonight. Before then, he has the usual daily Mass followed by a meeting with the parish building committee. Although he feels like he has no time for that meeting, he is, nonetheless, excited about it because they will be planning the big dedication ceremony for the new church. For Fr. Ron, building this new church—the largest and the most beautiful in the whole diocese—has been the greatest accomplishment of his priesthood thus far. "All for the glory of God," he keeps telling himself.

As if all that were not enough, this whole week has been filled with meetings outside the parish. Fr. Ron had meetings with the presbyteral council, the diocesan school board, and the capital campaign committee. He knew that he was taking on too much when he said, "Yes" to being part of all this, but since he has the reputation of having good business acumen (he earned an M.B.A. before entering the seminary), as well as much practical wisdom to share based on his experience building the new church, he just could not say, "No." He sees all these commitments as his way of being useful to the diocese.

Indeed, Fr. Ron has always placed a high value on being useful. He is glad that as a priest, he can help so many people as he does important things like celebrating the Sacraments, preaching, teaching, and visiting the sick. He only wishes that he could be even more productive so that he could accomplish even more in any given day. While the people frequently express their admiration at how much he does get done on a daily basis, he strangely feels like he is never really doing enough; there is always more that could be done.

As Fr. Ron lies in his bed with these thoughts flashing through his mind, feelings of emptiness and loneliness begin to emerge. Fr. Ron quickly pushes away these feelings. He gets up, brews a cup of coffee, and goes into the rectory chapel, resolving to get back to the practice of a daily Holy

Hour. But, as he sits down to pray, his mind starts racing about tonight's youth minister conference, and he ends up spending the whole hour writing his talk. He regrets not having had more of a heart-to-heart conversation with the Lord, but at least he is happy with his talk and he knows the people will love it.

Functionalism and the Contemporary Diocesan Priesthood

Father Ron is clearly a good and very gifted man who wants to help people. But there is something wrong. In the midst of all his good and important activity, he feels a great emptiness inside. This emptiness is a signal that this priest is afflicted with the disease of functionalism. A functionalist priest derives his identity from his activity, his work, his success, his titles, his rewards, his achievements, his fidelity to his duties, and other such externally based things. The problem here is not that Fr. Ron has built an amazing church building and that he is serving on these various boards—those things could be great contributions in the life of the Church—the problem is that Fr. Ron seems to be basing his *identity* on these achievements. He sees himself as successful, productive, and useful. Since the "self" or the "ego" seems to be the driving factor behind these accomplishments, he finds that he is doing all of this good work on his own, in isolation, apart from the Lord. The evidence that he is working in isolation is that Fr. Ron feels empty and lonely. Even Fr. Ron's Holy Hour has become utilitarian—rather than seeking the Lord's help through prayer, he spends his precious Holy Hour doing more work, all on his own.

Priests like Father Ron who are living in functionalism believe certain interior lies. For example: "I have to *do more* in

order to feel like my life has meaning;" "I need to build something;" "I am important because I have a title or am on many
boards and committees;" "I cannot afford to fail at anything;"
"I need to impress people with this talk or homily;" "my next
assignment has to be even more important than this one;" "I
have no time to pray because there is too much to do." These
lies are deeply rooted—they affect the priest on the level of
his identity.

It seems that the Congregation for the Clergy was speaking directly to priests like Fr. Ron when it published its *Directory on the Ministry and Life of Priests* in 1994:

> Pastoral charity faces the danger, today especially,
> of being emptied of its meaning through so-called
> "functionalism." It is not rare, in fact, to perceive, even
> in some priests, the influence of an erroneous mentality
> which reduces the ministerial priesthood to strictly
> functional aspects. To merely play the role of the priest,
> carrying out a few services and ensuring completion of
> various tasks would make up the entire priestly existence.
> Such a reductive conception of the identity of the
> ministry of the priest risks pushing their lives towards an
> emptiness, an emptiness which often comes to be filled by
> lifestyles not consonant with their very ministry.[2]

According to the Congregation for the Clergy, functionalism obscures the identity of the priest by placing the emphasis not on who a priest *is* but on what he *does*. For that reason,
a priest who is living out of a functionalist mentality places
a strong value on being productive and useful. In an article
written in 1999, Fr. William Sheridan asserts that the problem
of functionalism is rooted in the culture at large:

Functionalism pervades our culture. There is a tendency to measure things, ideas, and even people by what they do or what they produce. Our culture values usefulness over essence and the bottom line over the human person.[3]

A functional approach to priesthood can leave a priest feeling as though his existence is meaningless. In the words of Sheridan, "A priesthood based solely on what one does cannot truly satisfy a man as a human being."[4] As Fr. Mark O'Keefe says, if a priest desires a sense of fulfillment, then priestly identity cannot be located chiefly in the functions a priest performs: "I suspect that few priests have a sense, an experience, an intuition of their own identity, such that they could be satisfied by having their priestly identity understood to reside primarily in any function, no matter how sacred."[5]

Deacon James Keating makes the point that functionalism occurs when a priest neglects his interior life and draws only from his own resources. This self-reliance leads to a surface level existence wherein the priest finds it hard to cope with what seems like an almost unbearable routine:

> . . . [the priest's] ministry simply becomes a function, a series of familiar exercises repeating themselves over time, albeit dressed in differing circumstances from year to year. . . . As with any life commitment, familiarity can breed a superficial and distracting longing for the novel.[6]

When the priest takes on this way of thinking, he can easily fall prey to the "voices" of the "culture of distraction."[7] This "longing for the novel" could lead the priest into dangerous habits and vices.

Due to its gravity, functionalism can be considered a "disease." Pope Francis used this type of language in an address to Cardinals and Superiors of the Roman Curia. The Holy Father linked functionalism to a conception of the priesthood that is more businesslike than apostolic. Pope Francis said, "*The sickness of excessive planning and functionalism: When the apostle plans everything minutely and thinks that with perfect planning things effectively progress, thus becoming an accountant or a businessman.*"[8] One of the dangers of reducing the priesthood merely to being a business is that the priest falls "into the temptation of wanting to enclose and pilot the freedom of the Holy Spirit who remains always greater, more generous than any human planning (Cf. *John* 3:8)."[9]

Consequences of Functionalism

When left unchecked, functionalism can quickly become careerism. If a priest is basing his identity on his achievements and titles, then it is understandable that he will want to "climb the ladder" in order to gain further recognition. This trajectory can be seen in the vignette of Fr. Ron. It is easy to imagine him thinking, "Now that I am on these various boards and have accomplished so much, surely I will be noticed. Perhaps I will receive the title of Monsignor, and maybe even be made a bishop someday."

Pope Francis has frequently decried careerism among priests throughout his pontificate. For example, in an address to students of the Pontifical Ecclesiastical Academy, Francis exhorted the students to be free from "personal projects," from "the possibility of planning [their] future," from "ambitions," and from seeking "recognition" from their work. He strongly summed up these exhortations by warning, "Careerism is a form of leprosy, a leprosy. No careerism, please."[10]

Another consequence of functionalism is workaholism. If a priest is seeking his identity based on his work, especially if there is a hope of "advancing his career," it should not be surprising that he becomes addicted to his work. Dr. Barbara Killinger, a psychologist, defines a workaholic as a "work-obsessed individual who gradually becomes *emotionally crippled* and addicted to power and control in a compulsive drive to gain approval and public recognition of success."[11] The workaholic is fixated on gaining the approval of others and is endlessly seeking success as a means to gain that approval. "These driven men and women live a Gerbil-wheel, adrenalin-pumping existence rushing from plan A to B, narrowly-fixated on some ambitious goal or accomplishment. Eventually, nothing or no one else really matters."[12] A key word here is "driven." There is a big difference between a priest who is *driven* by his ego and a priest who is, instead, *led* by the Holy Spirit.

One further consequence of functionalism is that it can lead to the question of whether or not priests are even needed at all. This is the argument made by Paul Josef Cardinal Cordes in commenting on Hans Küng's work, *Why Priests?*[13] Cordes writes, "His [Küng's] observations on the priesthood are guided exclusively by the question of its purpose and center on the activity to which the priest must dedicate himself. In the final analysis, he summarizes this within the task of 'guiding the community,' exercised under the form of multiple 'functions.'"[14]

Cordes asserts that rather than being "a help," Küng's work is more of a "dead end."[15] Küng's work is a dead end because he envisions the priesthood as connected solely with functionalism in the form of utilitarianism. As Cordes puts it:

> . . . the direction suggested by Professor Küng brings to light a fundamental error: from the time of his writing even to this day, there has been the attempt to define priestly identity on a purely utilitarian basis. The focus is on the role and purpose of the priest. The priest's mission in and for the Church must be assured—precisely within a system of functionality. Functionality corresponds undoubtedly to the modern mentality.[16]

According to Cordes, if the focus is on the role and purpose of the priest, then the priest can be replaced by a layperson who leads a parish community. When that happens, "Professional consultants—not pastors of souls—become the guiding figures for the salvation of souls."[17] And the problem is then an obscuring of priestly identity: "As soon as functions become interchangeable, then the true nature of the priesthood is confused."[18]

Priestly Identity and Communion with Christ

The central issue, then, is one of identity. A priest living in functionalism is basing his identity on what he *does* rather than on who he *is*. He must realize that before he *does* anything, before he functions as a priest, he already *is* a priest. Cardinal Timothy Dolan expresses it this way:

> On the day before I was ordained a priest, I went to confession to a Paraclete Father in St. Louis. He asked me what I looked forward to in the priesthood. Of course I answered, predictably, "Offering Mass, hearing confessions, serving people in a parish," and so on.

"Excellent," my confessor responded, "but enjoy as well being a priest. You know, if you were in an automobile accident the day after your First Mass and were paralyzed completely, meaning you could not ever do any of the things ordinarily associated with priestly ministry, you would still be a priest." And then words I'll never forget, he said, "Spend time every day acknowledging that priestly identity, rejoicing in it, nourishing it, thanking God for it—and then what you do as a priest will be all the more effective and rewarding, because it flows from who you are." Now that's what I mean by priestly identity.[19]

The principle being expressed here is the Scholastic axiom *agere sequitur esse*—action follows being.[20] A priest's very *being* has been indelibly marked by the Sacrament of Holy Orders. As Fr. David Toups describes it, "The priest must know that the gift received at ordination permanently marks his soul and draws him into a unique union with Jesus Christ the Head and Shepherd of the Church. The priest's union with the High Priest is so profound it is ontological."[21]

This reality of the primacy of *being* over *doing* with regard to the priesthood can be seen in a particularly striking way in the lives of priests who are cloistered monks. For example, a Carthusian[22] priest might, on occasion, be the main celebrant at Mass for the community and, perhaps, hear an occasional confession, but for the most part he is not "doing" specifically priestly things in his daily life—his work is mainly manual labor like the other brothers. Yet, his priesthood has immense value in and of itself—his soul has been configured to Christ the High Priest through the Sacrament of Holy

Orders, and this reality magnifies even further the salvific fruitfulness of his vocation to a life of prayer.[23]

While a diocesan priest has a rather different vocation than that of a Carthusian priest, he can—nevertheless— receive the consoling truth that even if a priest *does* nothing seemingly useful in the eyes of the world, he *is* still a priest in his very being and, thus, his life is immensely fruitful and valuable even apart from his functions. This truth can help to dispel functionalism insofar as it helps the priest to realize that his identity need not be rooted in his activities or achievements. The priest can then find greater freedom in letting go of excess activity, especially any ministry that he has taken on apart from Christ in order to satisfy the needs of his own ego.

This realization can help the priest appreciate the words of Servant of God Catherine de Hueck Doherty who, in her spiritual work *Poustinia: Encountering God in Silence, Solitude, and Prayer*, lamented the tendency of western culture to focus on productivity and suggested another approach to the priesthood:

> The West values itself for its ability to produce things. Priests, nuns and lay people tend to evaluate themselves interiorly by what they can *produce*. Priests especially do not realize that their presence is enough. I often tell priests who work in parishes that one of the best things they can "do" is simply walk around their neighborhood and be present to their people. But if they aren't doing something, they feel that they are wasting their lives away.[24]

What the Russian baroness is conveying is that the priest's presence is enough because he is already ontologically united to Jesus Christ in his very being. That means that when a priest is present, he brings not only himself but the priestly presence of Christ.

As amazing as this truth is, merely appreciating and recognizing the value of his own "being" as a priest is not enough to completely dispel functionalism once and for all. In his human weakness, the priest could easily forget or over-look the reality of his ontological union with Christ. He could easily slip into "autopilot" mode, acting on his own, apart from Christ. This is especially true for the diocesan priest who has a full load of legitimate ministerial activity that needs to be accomplished if he is to be faithful to his vocation.[25] The diocesan priest is called to celebrate Mass, preach, teach, hear confessions, visit the sick, go to parish council meetings, serve on various committees as needed, accept invitations to speaking engagements when properly discerned, and so on. With all that is on his plate and in his human weakness, the priest can easily be consumed by these activities to the point where he is tempted to find his identity through his success in these endeavors.

Therefore, the only antidote to the disease of functional-ism is for the priest consciously to seek to be in communion with Christ in all that he does. In other words, the priest is called to *do* his ministry, but to do it in communion with Christ, and do only what the Father wants him to do. His sense of joy and fulfillment will come only through living every moment of his life in communion with Christ. This joy and fulfillment flows from the fact that when he is in communion with Christ, the priest discovers that he is able to receive God's love for him even in the very midst of his apostolic activity. He recognizes the refreshing truth of St. Catherine of Siena's powerful image of continously drinking from the fountain of God's love: "If a man carry away the vessel which he has filled at the fountain and then drink of it, the vessel becomes empty, but if he keep his vessel standing in the fountain, while he drinks, it always remains full."[26] When the priest keeps his vessel constantly in the fountain, he is able to receive God's love as he is giving God's love; and his own cup never goes empty. The priest is then constantly energized, even in the midst of his ministry, as he receives what own his heart is most longing for. In the beautiful words of the *Imitation of Christ*, "Until you are intimately united with Christ, you will never find your true rest."[27]

Most importantly, it is only in communion with Christ that the priest's true identity is found. As St. John Paul II puts it, "The priest finds the full truth of his identity in being a derivation, a specific participation in and continuation of Christ himself, the one high priest of the new and eternal covenant."[28] The priest is not simply a functionary, bringing his own gifts and talents to the Church; rather, what the priest brings is Christ Himself. The priest is a "living image of Jesus Christ."[29] When the priest is grounded in his true identity in Christ, he will be less likely to try to find his identity through his activity or achievements.

That the antidote to the disease of functionalism is communion with Christ can be clearly seen in the writings of Pope Benedict XVI. In an essay entitled "The Ministry and Life of Priests," written before his election to the papacy, Benedict begins by describing the emptiness that results from functionalism. He presents the issue rather starkly, and it is well worth quoting him at length. He is commenting on the decree *Presbyterorum Ordinis* of the Second Vatican Council, which, he said:

> . . . speaks of the difficult problem of the interior unity of his life that the priest has to deal with when he is faced with a great number of different tasks; it is a problem which, with the continuing decline in the number of priests, threatens to become ever more the real crisis of priestly existence. A pastor today, who is in charge of three or four parishes, and always on the move from one place to another, a situation that the missionaries know well, is becoming more the norm for the countries of ancient Christianity. The priest, who must try to guarantee the celebration of the sacraments in the communities, is tormented by administrative duties, is challenged by the complexity of every kind of question, and is aware of the difficulties of persons that he does not even have the time to contact. Torn between the variety of activities, the priest becomes drained and finds fewer opportunities for recollection, which would give him the new energy and inspiration. Externally stretched and interiorly drained, he loses the joy of his vocation, which in the end he feels to be an unbearable burden. There is nothing left but flight.[30]

The solution for Benedict XVI to the emptiness that results from functionalism is what he describes as "intimate communion with Christ whose food was to do the will of the Father (Jn 4:34)."[31] Benedict asserts:

> It is important that the ontological union with Christ abide in the conscience and in action: all that I do, I

am doing in communion with Him. By doing it, I am with Him. All my activities, no matter how varied and often externally divergent, constitute only one vocation: to be together with Christ acting as an instrument in communion with Him.[32]

Pope Benedict's words show us that when a priest is living in this intimate communion with Christ, he is able to engage in a lot of activity without being defined by this activity. Such a priest can work hard without becoming a workaholic or functionalist because his identity is centered in Christ and not in his work.[33]

Jesus Christ: Communion Incarnate

When we look at Jesus Christ, we see that the focal point of His life was and is His constant communion with the Father, to such an extent that Jesus can be thought of as "Communion Incarnate." It is impossible for us to imagine a functionalist Jesus, deriving His identity from His activities and accomplishments. As He walked this earth, Jesus knew who He was before He *did* anything—He was (and is) Son of God. His identity was received through His relationship with the Father. Only the Father could tell Him who He was. Indeed, Pope Benedict XVI points out that the title "Son" is the summation of Jesus' identity. While the infant Church had a plethora of titles for Jesus, a concentration eventually took place: " . . . the title 'Son' comes in the end to be the only, comprehensive designation for Jesus. It both comprises and interprets everything else."[34] The simple title "Son" reveals who Jesus is: a person who is in relation with His Father.

In fact, Jesus Christ lives in relation to the Father to such a degree that Pope Benedict wrote that Jesus is "pure relation"[35] with the Father. Benedict describes this relationality in a profound way:

> The Son as Son, and insofar as he is Son, does not proceed in any way from himself and so is completely one with the Father; since he is nothing beside him, claims no special position of his own, confronts the Father with nothing belonging only to him, makes no reservations for what is specifically his own, therefore he is completely equal to the Father. The logic is compelling: If there is nothing in which he is just he, no kind of fenced-off private ground, then he coincides with the Father.[36]

Even as Jesus lives in oneness with the Father, He, nevertheless, needs to be in constant conversation with the Father. His own ontological unity with the Father needs to be lived out subjectively. Pope Benedict uses the word "communication" to describe this dynamic: "According to the testimony of Holy Scripture, the center of the life and person of Jesus is his constant communication with the Father."[37] Benedict's words indicate that Jesus' relationship with the Father is dynamic rather than static. Jesus is not merely aware of who He is ontologically as Son; but as Son, He is in constant *dialogue* with the Father. For that reason, Jesus often went into solitude to speak to and listen to the Father. Benedict writes, " . . . the entire gospel testimony is unanimous that Jesus' words and deeds flows [sic] from his most intimate communion with the Father; that he continually went 'into the hills' to pray in solitude after the burden of the day."[38] As an example, Jesus called the Twelve Apostles only after spending the night in prayer to the Father.[39] As Benedict puts it, "the calling of the Twelve proceeds from prayer, from the Son's converse with the Father. The Church is born in that prayer in which Jesus gives himself back into the Father's hands and the Father commits everything to the Son."[40]

Unlike a functionalist, Jesus did not do everything that the people wanted Him to do. When, as a result of the many healings and deliverances He had worked, Jesus was told, "Everyone is looking for you," His response was, "Let us go on to the nearby villages that I may preach there also" (Mk 1:37-38). Jesus' response shows that He lived in great freedom because He listened only to the Father's voice. In the midst of all that He did on this earth, He lived in constant communion with the Father. In that way, while His life was full of activity, He did not derive His identity from these activities, but only from who He knew Himself to be as Son of God.

Relationship, Identity, Mission

Just as Jesus was in constant communion with the Father and received His very identity from this relationship with the Father, so the priest must live in constant communion with Jesus in order to discover and live out of his own identity. When the priest knows his identity, he will also know what his mission is. As Fr. Richard Gabuzda puts it, the correct approach is Relationship, Identity, Mission (R.I.M.).[41] When the priest is living in communion or relationship with Jesus, he knows his identity in Christ as a son in the Son. Only when the priest is grounded in his identity can he, then, be sent on mission. To get this approach backwards and place one's mission first and seek to derive one's identity from that mission is to fall into functionalism and all of its negative consequences.

NOTES

1.   This is a fictional account. Although this vignette is exaggerated, it reflects the real-life struggles of many priests who can probably identify with at least some element of this example.

2.   Congregation for the Clergy, *Directory on the Ministry and Life of Priests* (1994), sec. 44, accessed July 11, 2015, http://www.vatican.va/roman_curia/congregations/cclergy/documents/rc_con_cclergy_doc_31011994_directory_en.html.

3.   William P. Sheridan, "Functionalism Undermining Priesthood," *Human Development* 20.3 (Fall 1999): 12.

4.   Ibid.

5.   Mark O'Keefe, *In Persona Christi* (Meinrad, IN: St. Meinrad School of Theology, 1998), 5.

6.   James Keating, "Priestly Formation as Spirituality," *Sacrum Ministerium* 15 (Feb. 2009): 102.

7.   James Keating, "The Logos in Seminary Formation and Teaching," March 5, 2011, accessed August 26, 2017, http://www.ignatiusinsight.com/features2011/jkeating_logosandformation_mar2011.asp.

8.   Francis, "Pope's Address to Roman Curia," *Zenit: The World Seen from Rome*, December 23, 2014, accessed January 1, 2015, http://www.zenit.org/en/articles/pope-s-address-to-roman-curia. Emphasis added.

9.   Ibid.

10.   Francis, *Address of Pope Francis to the Community of the Pontifical Ecclesiastical Academy*, accessed August 3, 2017, https://w2.vatican.va/content/francesco/en/speeches/2013/june/documents/papa-francesco_20130606_pontificia-accademia-ecclesiastica.html.

11.   Barbara Killinger, "Understanding the Dynamics of Workaholism: Are You a Workaholic?" December 15, 2011, accessed May 7, 2015, https://www.psychologytoday.com/blog/the-workaholics/201112/understanding-the-dynamics-workaholism.

12.   Ibid.

13.   Hans Küng, *Why Priests? A Proposal for a New Church Ministry* (New York: Doubleday & Co., 1971).

14.   Paul Josef Cardinal Cordes, *The Priest: Irreplaceable in the Church's Mission* (lecture given to the priests of the Diocese of Phoenix, Phoenix, Arizona, 1 December 2014), 3. See also Paul Josef Cardinal Cordes, *Why Priests? Answers Guided by the Teaching of Benedict XVI*, trans. Peter Spring and Anthony J. Figueiredo (New York: Scepter Publishers, 2009).

15.   Ibid., 4.

16.   Ibid.

17.   Ibid., 5.

18.   Ibid.

19.   Timothy M. Dolan, *Priests for the Third Millenium* (Huntington, IN.: Our Sunday Visitor, Inc., 2000), 228-229.

20.   Ibid., 228.

21.   David L. Toups, *Reclaiming Our Priestly Character* (Omaha, NE: The Institute for Priestly Formation, 2008), 32.

22.   The Carthusian Order, founded by St. Bruno (1030-1101), is often considered to be the strictest of all monastic communities. The monks live in the solitude of their own cells while coming together only for Mass, Night Vigils, and Vespers. They have no external apostolate whatsoever.

23.   Incidentally, even a Carthusian priest can be tempted toward functionalism, only from a different starting point. He might think, "Look how needed my priestly ministry is 'out there,' especially with the priest shortage. Here I am, simply praying and chopping wood. Wouldn't I be more effective and valuable if I were out there helping the people?"

24.   Catherine de Hueck Doherty, *Poustinia: Encountering God in Silence, Solitude, and Prayer*, 3rd ed. (Combermere, Ontario: Madonna House Publications, 2009), 47.

25.   St. Francis de Sales makes the point that a person's spiritual life must correspond with his or her actual state in life. He asks, " . . . would it be fitting that a Bishop should seek to lead the solitary life of a Carthusian?" See Saint Francis de Sales, *Introduction to the Devout Life*, with a Preface by Edward M. Egan (New York: Vintage Spiritual Classics, 2002), 7.

26.   St. Catherine of Siena, *The Dialogue of St. Catherine of Siena* (New York: Cosimo Classics, 2007), 155. This is from the section, *A Treatise of Discretion*, no. 49.

27.   *The Imitation of Christ*, Lib. 2, 1-6, quoted in *The Liturgy of the Hours, Ordinary Time, Weeks 1-17* (New York: Catholic Book Publishing Co., 1975), 528. The author goes on to say, "Once you have entered completely into the depths of Jesus, and have a taste of his powerful love, then you will not care about your own convenience or inconvenience."

28.   John Paul II, *Pastores Dabo Vobis* (Boston: Pauline Books and Media, 1992), sec. 12.

29.   Ibid., sec. 22.

30.   Joseph Ratzinger, "Life and Ministry of Priests," in *Priesthood: A Greater Love—International Symposium on the Thirtieth Anniversary of the Promulgation of the Conciliar Decree Presbyterorum Ordinis*, 28 October 1995 (Philadelphia: Archdiocese of Philadelphia, 1997), 126.

31.   Ibid.

32.   Ibid. Incidentally, at least in the way this text is translated, Benedict seems to make a distinction between the words "union" and "communion." He says that the priest's ontological *union* with Christ needs to abide in his conscience in such a way that the priest lives in *communion* with Christ. Webster's dictionary defines union as "an act or instance of uniting or joining two or more things into one" (https://www.merriam-webster.

com/dictionary/union). Webster's defines communion as "an act or instance of sharing" or "intimate fellowship or support" (https://www. merriam-webster.com/dictionary/communion). While the words are pointing to the same reality, there are subtle differences in connotation. The word union means "oneness," whereas communion (literally "with oneness") has more of a connotation of "togetherness" or "fellowship." While the Church's Tradition seems to use the words union and communion interchangeably, and they do point to the same reality, it is important to note the distinctions.

33.   As Killinger puts it from a secular point of view, "'*What is the difference between a hard worker and a workaholic?*' is a frequently asked question. A hard worker who is *emotionally present* for all family members, co-workers and friends, and who manages to maintain a healthy balance between work and personal responsibility is *not* a workaholic." It is this emotional presence to other people that makes all the difference. For our purposes, it could be said that a priest who is emotionally present to Jesus Christ—in other words, living in intimate communion with Him—and, thus, emotionally present to the people he serves—can work hard without being considered a workaholic (Killinger, "Workaholism").

34.   Joseph Ratzinger, *Behold the Pierced One: An Approach to a Spiritual Christology*, trans. Graham Harrison (San Francisco: Ignatius Press, 1986), 16.

35.   Joseph Ratzinger, *Introduction to Christianity*, trans. J.R. Foster, with a new Preface trans. Michael J. Miller (San Francisco: Ignatius Press, 1968, 2004), 186.

36.   Ibid., 186.

37.   Ratzinger, *Behold the Pierced One*, 15.

38.   Ibid., 17-19.

39.   See Luke 6:12-16.

40.   Ratzinger, *Behold the Pierced One*, 18.

41.   Richard J. Gabuzda, "Relationship, Identity, Mission: A Proposal for Spiritual Formation," paper presented at the Fourth Annual Symposium on the Spirituality and Identity of the Diocesan Priest entitled *Interiority for Mission: Spiritual Formation for Priests of the New Evangelization*, St. John Vianney Theological Seminary, Denver, Colorado, 2-6 March 2005, 39-51.

BLESSED COLUMBA MARMION
TOUCHING GOD

In an effort to arrive at a greater understanding of what "communion with Christ" means, it is helpful to look at the writings of Blessed Columba Marmion. Although Marmion was a Benedictine monk and abbot, he gave many retreats to diocesan priests on the subject of communion with Christ. He understood the life of diocesan priests well because he was initially a diocesan priest himself before discerning a call to the monastic life.

Blessed Columba Marmion was ordained a priest in 1881 and served for one year as a parish priest in Dundrum, which is near Dublin in Ireland.[1] After this period of parochial ministry, he was appointed as the chair of the philosophy department at the seminary in Clonliffe. During the four years that he served in the seminary, many seminarians came to him for spiritual direction. In addition to his other duties, he served as chaplain to two communities of nuns and also worked in prison ministry in Dublin.

Marmion had long desired to live as a monk, and his dream became a reality in 1886 when he entered the Benedictine Abbey of Maredsous at the age of twenty-eight. He was quickly sought after for spiritual guidance by local parish priests. He began an apostolate for priests by way of recollections that were given to the clergy every month for two years. This ministry for priests flourished after he was sent to Louvain in 1899, where he served for ten years in university and seminary work.

One of Marmion's most famous spiritual directees was Monsignor—and later Cardinal—Mercier. According to Dom Mark Tierney, who was Marmion's biographer, when Cardinal Mercier was asked what it was that made Marmion's books so popular, Mercier replied, "He makes you touch God."[2] He elaborated, "Marmion had a special charism, which he proffered with a gentle touch, to bring people closer to God."[3] Since Marmion's charism benefitted priests in particular, his insights are especially important in helping priests today to "touch God," that is, to be in communion with Him.

Blessed Marmion saw communion with Christ as essential to the life of the priest. This truth can be seen clearly in his treatise *Christ the Ideal of the Priest* where Marmion says, "The one deep, durable joy of this life is to be found in union with God. This is true for all men, but it is a thousand times truer for the priest."[4] Marmion knew that priests, like everyone, can often be tempted to seek happiness in other places. But according to Marmion, "It is in vain for him [the priest] to try to quench his thirst for happiness by drinking at other springs; his heart has been consecrated to Christ and can find its rest only in charity . . . Jesus is everything for us."[5] It is only when priests today recognize that "Jesus is everything" for them and, thus, choose to live in communion with Him that they will find the happiness for which they long.

Marmion mentions several priest saints—St. Benedict, St. Francis Xavier, St. Charles Borromeo, St. Francis de Sales, St.

Alphonsus Ligouri, and St. John Vianney—who were very active and "accomplished great things for love of God," but emphasizes that "they were also men of prayer . . . they all spent hours conversing with God."[6] As it was for them, so it must be for priests today; and, therefore, Marmion gives the exhortation, "Let us be, therefore, mediators conscious of our mission, men of prayer who, by virtue of our constant communion with the Lord, sanctify the souls of which we have charge, while at the same time sanctifying ourselves."[7] From these words, it is clear that in Marmion's view, priests need to be in "constant communion with the Lord," and this is connected with being "men of prayer." Since prayer is so essential to being in constant communion with the Lord, it will be helpful to look specifically at Marmion's articulation of prayer in order to arrive at a clearer understanding of what "communion with Christ" means.

Of all of Marmion's major works, *Christ, the Life of the Soul* is the work in which Marmion speaks of prayer most extensively. "Praying is one of the most necessary means for bringing about, here below, our union with God and our imitation of Christ Jesus."[8] What becomes clear from Marmion's words is that communion with God is not merely the result of the Sacraments, but something that needs to be subjectively appropriated by way of prayer. Marmion writes, ". . . prayer keeps the soul in frequent contact with God; it establishes, and having established keeps going, a fire-hearth in the soul . . ."[9] Here, we find a helpful "definition" of communion with Christ as "contact" with Him. The image of a fire-hearth speaks to the fact that this communion with God, or "contact" with Him, is a tangible reality that one can experience in the soul.

Communion with God is such a tangible reality that it is experienced on the level of the affect, in such a way that "the heart . . . [is] . . . filled with *feelings* of faith, reverence, humility, ardent trust, generous love," as one listens to God in prayer.[10] Marmion quotes St. Francis de Sales in saying that prayer enables the soul to be "united with God through *feelings* and communications that all the words and wisdom of men are unable to effect without Him."[11] Again, the fact that feelings are involved means that this union with God is a perceptible reality that one can experience.

It should be noted that even though Marmion is emphasizing the role of feelings in an effort to make clear that communion with Christ is something that can be tangibly experienced, it is also true that one's feelings may not always be activated when living in this communion. It is here that the role of faith becomes so critical. As Fr. Tadeusz Dajczer puts it, in words reminiscent of St. John of the Cross, "True faith is free from all natural supports such as understanding, feelings, and intellectual or imaginative experiences. True faith is dependent solely on Him and on His word."[12] As Marmion himself says, " . . . faith is the first virtue that Our Lord requires of those who approach Him."[13] When a person is not experiencing God on the level of the affect, this gives him or her a chance to grow in faith by *seeking* God. As Dajczer describes it, "Growth of faith will be indicated by your *increasingly intense looking for God to come and your hungering for Him.*"[14]

When God does come to us, He often brings with Him a feeling of His presence; that is the nature of who God is as Love. The tendency of many priests is to withhold themselves from the Lord, sometimes because of a false assumption that they are not supposed to habitually "feel" Him. However, God may want us to feel His presence more than we think. As St. Paul says in his speech to the Athenians in the Acts of the Apostles, God created men "that people might seek God, perhaps even grope for him and find him" (Acts 17:27). Even mystical writers like St. John of the Cross, who often caution against being overly attached to feelings, nevertheless emphasize that feelings are a part of the spiritual life, especially as one's union with God grows. For example, in speaking of the "living flame of love" that is God's presence in the soul, St. John of the Cross says, "The soul *feels* this [living flame] and speaks of it thus . . . with intimate and delicate sweetness of love, burning in love's flame . . . ."[15]

In speaking of the connection between prayer and feelings, Marmion is not referring to feelings as merely passing emotions. Rather, he is referring to the necessity of the *will* being "stirred into flame." Marmion says that, "Prayer does not really commence until the time when the will, stirred into flame, makes super-natural contact with Divine Good through affection and abandons itself to Him through love, so as to please Him, so as to carry out His precepts and His desires."[16] In other words, feelings or affections are important because they are connected to the will which, as a faculty of the soul, is essential to the life of prayer.

One of the reasons why many priests do not have a more tangible sense of the Lord's presence is that their prayer is too often in the "head" and not enough in the "heart." According to Marmion, prayer takes place primarily in the heart: "It is in the heart that prayer essentially resides."[17] Pope Benedict XVI echoes this sentiment when he writes, "The organ for seeing God is the heart. The intellect alone is not enough."[18] To further explicate this reality of prayer residing in the heart, Marmion gives the example of the Blessed Virgin Mary, as well as Christ's own teaching on prayer:

> It is said of the Virgin Mary that she kept the words of Jesus "in her heart;" it is there, indeed—never forget it—that prayer fundamentally has its lodging-place. When Our Lord taught His Apostles to pray, He did not say: "Engage in this or that reasoning," but "Express the affection of your hearts as children:" "In this manner . . . shall you pray: 'Our Father . . . hallowed be thy name.'"[19]

Indeed, for Marmion, the recognition that one is a child of God is essential to the Christian life, so much so that the doctrine of the "Divine Adoption" is the central core of Marmion's spiritual teachings.[20] Thus, Marmion tells us that prayer is simply "a conversation of a child of God with its heavenly Father."[21] In describing this filial and conversational nature of prayer, Marmion quotes the great St. Teresa of Avila: "Such is mental prayer: a heart-to-heart between God and the soul: 'a conversation, person to person, with God, to express our love to Him who we know loves us.'"[22]

It is in this context of the Divine adoption that Marmion again emphasizes the role of feelings. Marmion writes, "Prayer is . . . the flowering, under the action of the gifts of the Holy Spirit, of the feelings that result from our divine adoption in Jesus Christ; and that is why it has to be accessible to every baptized soul of good will."[23] To express it another way, part of prayer is experiencing on the level of feelings that one is a child of God. This further confirms that communion with Christ, which takes us up into Christ's own

Sonship before the Father, can often be experienced on the level of the affections.

This communion with Christ is something that one can begin to experience in an increasingly profound way. That is the claim Marmion makes in speaking of the illuminative stage[24] of the spiritual life:

> The soul, in return, constantly translates its feelings into acts of faith, of repentance, of compunction, of trust, of love, of taking pleasure [in God], of *abandon* to the will of the Father. It moves as in an atmosphere that keeps it, more and more, in union with God; prayer becomes as it were its breath, its life; it is filled with the spirit of prayer. Prayer becomes then a *state*, and the soul can find its God whenever it wishes, even in the midst of all its occupations.[25]

This movement of the soul involves abandonment to the Father's will.[26] Living this way enables the priest to "find God in all things."[27] It is so important for the priest to see that this communion is meant to be there for the priest not only in his formal times of prayer, but always:

> Those times of the day that a soul devotes exclusively to the formal *exercise* of prayer are but an intensification of this state, in which the soul stays, habitually but sweetly, united to God in order to speak to Him from its inner self, and in turn to listen to the voice from on high.[28]

In other words, there is a "sweetness" that accompanies this union with God, and this union involves a continual conversation with God. Marmion further elucidates this point in a beautiful way:

This state is more than the simple presence of God; it is an inner conversation, full of love, in which the soul speaks to God—sometimes with the lips, but more often it is the heart that speaks—and in which the soul stays intimately united with Him, despite the labors and the occupations of the day. There are many simple and upright souls who, faithful to the attracting of the Holy Spirit, arrive at this state that is so desirable.[29]

It is important to note that this union with God, which is accessible to "simple and upright souls," is something that is very intimate. God desires that his priests live intimately united with Him in the midst of all their occupations and activities. This intimacy with God is a state in which the soul "feels itself united"[30] with God and " . . . tastes the happiness of staying there before God."[31]

To sum up, Blessed Columba Marmion's writings on prayer teach us that communion with God can be defined as "contact" with God or "touching" God. This contact with God, while having faith as its "foundation,"[32] is something very tangible insofar as it occurs on the level of the affect. According to Marmion, a person can feel himself to be united with God, and there is even a certain sweetness to this communion.[33] Most importantly, communion also involves an ongoing conversation with God as a child to its father. It is this ongoing conversation that helps keep a person connected with God and in a state of abandonment to the Father's will.

NOTES

1.   Columba Marmion, *Christ: The Ideal of the Priest* (San Francisco: Ignatius, 2005), 11. All the biographical data on Marmion in this paragraph and the following paragraph comes from this source.

2.   Mark Tierney, "Introduction," in Columba Marmion, *Christ: The Life of the Soul* (San Francisco: Ignatius, 2005), xiii.

3.   Ibid.

4.   Marmion, *Ideal*, 179.

5.   Ibid.

6.   Ibid., 283.

7.   Ibid. Emphasis added.

8.   Marmion, *Soul*, 415.

9.   Ibid.

10.   Ibid., 423. Emphasis added.

11.   Ibid., 424-425. Emphasis added.

12.   Tadeusz Dajczer, *The Gift of Faith,* 3rd ed. (Fort Collins, CO: In the Arms of Mary Foundation, 2012), 109.

13.   Marmion, *Soul*, 175.

14.   Dajczer, *The Gift of Faith*, 110-111. Emphasis in the original.

15.   St. John of the Cross, "The Living Flame of Love," in *The Collected Works of St. John of the Cross,* trans. Kieran Kavanaugh and Otilio Rodriguez, revised ed. (Washington, D.C.: ICS Publications, 1991), no. 4, p. 639.

16.   Marmion, *Soul*, 429.

17.   Ibid.

18.   Benedict XVI, *Jesus of Nazareth: From the Baptism in the Jordan to the Transfiguration*, trans. Adrian J. Walker (New York: Doubleday, 2007), 92.

19.   Marmion, *Soul*, 429.

20.   Ibid., xiii. Marmion's biographer, Dom Mark Tierney, writes here in the Introduction: "If one were to pinpoint the central theme of all Marmion's teaching, it could be summed up in the two words *Divine adoption.*"

21.   Ibid., 417.

22.   Teresa of Avila, *The Book of Her Life,* no. VIII, quoted in Marmion, *Soul*, 421.

23.   Marmion, *Soul*, 422-423.

24.   Following the theological tradition of the Purgative, Illuminative, and Unitive Ways. See, for example, Adolphe Tanquerrey, *The Spiritual Life* (Charlotte, NC: Tan Books, 2000), 297.

25.   Marmion, *Soul*, 435.

26.   For an excellent treatise on abandonment to God's will, see Jean Pierre de Caussade's classic *Abandonment to Divine Providence*, as well as a more contemporary work by Wilfrid Stinissen entitled *Into Your Hands*

Father: Abandoning Ourselves to the God Who Loves Us (San Francisco: Ignatius Press, 2011).

27.   This famous expression of St. Ignatius of Loyola is core to Ignatian Spirituality. St. Ignatius used this expression in a letter to Antonio Bandão, June 1, 1551, as cited by Timothy Gallagher in *The Examen Prayer: Ignatian Wisdom for Our Lives Today* (New York: The Crossroad Publishing Company, 2006), 179.

28.   Marmion, *Soul*, 435.

29.   Ibid.

30.   Ibid., 436.

31.   Ibid.

32.   Ibid., 179.

33.   While feelings may be involved in this communion, feelings are not what is essential, nor are they a proof that one has had a genuine mystical experience. A real mystical experience is known by its fruits, in the case of priests, namely pastoral charity. In other words, genuine mystical experience results in a greater spiritual fruitfulness—greater desire to give of oneself. For a further discussion of this point, see Moshe Idel and Bernard McGinn, eds., *Mystical Union in Judaism, Christianity, and Islam: An Ecumenical Dialogue Paperback* (New York: Continuum International Publishing Group, 1996), 14.

The Second Vatican Council
Sacrament of Holy Orders

The definition of communion with Christ that arises from Blessed Columba Marmion's teaching on prayer provides a solid basis for an even deeper theological exploration of communion with Christ in the life of the priest. A starting point for this deeper theological exploration will be the documents of the Second Vatican Council on the priesthood. Vatican II teaches us that the Sacrament of Holy Orders configures the priest to "Christ the head,"[1] yet this ontological union of the priest with Christ needs to be subjectively appropriated. As Fr. James Rafferty puts it, "The reception of ordination begs the priest each day to choose personal communion with the eternal High Priest as the central, irreplaceable, inviolable relationship of the priest's life."[2] This call for the priest to live in personal communion with Christ can be seen in the three primary documents of the Second Vatican Council that treat aspects of the priesthood: the *Dogmatic Constitution on the Church* (*Lumen Gentium*), the *Decree on the Training of Priests* (*Optatam Totius*), and the *Decree on the Ministry and Life of Priests* (*Presbyterorum Ordinis*).

Vatican II's *Dogmatic Constitution on the Church* (*Lumen Gentium*) makes an important distinction between the common priesthood of the faithful and the ministerial priesthood and, in so doing, raises the subject of priestly identity:

> Though they differ essentially and not only in degree, the common priesthood of the faithful and the ministerial or hierarchical priesthood are none the less ordered one to another; each in its own proper way shares in the one priesthood of Christ. The ministerial priest, by the sacred power that he has, forms and rules the priestly people; in the person of Christ he effects the Eucharistic sacrifice and offers it to God in the name of all the people.[3]

Here, we see the important term *"in persona Christi"*—the priest offers the Eucharist "in the person of Christ." What does *"in persona Christi"* mean? Archbishop Samuel Aquila offers a helpful explanation when he describes this phrase as meaning, " . . . a sacramental presence of Christ, for the people of God, which comes through the grace of the Holy Spirit in the Sacrament of Orders."[4] Aquila derives this explanation from St. John Paul II who says:

> The priest offers the holy sacrifice "in persona Christi;" this means more than offering "in the name of" or "in the place of" Christ. *In persona* means in specific sacramental identification with "the eternal High Priest" who is the Author and principal subject of this sacrifice of his, a sacrifice in which, in truth, nobody can take his place.[5]

In other words, *"in persona Christi"* means that the priest is sacramentally identified with Christ the eternal High Priest.[6]

This sacramental identification of the ministerial priest with Christ the High Priest implies an ontological union between the priest and Christ. While *Lumen Gentium* does not speak explicitly about this union,[7] the document does say that priests are called to holiness by way of an "overflowing contemplation," which helps priests to continue growing in holiness rather than to be hampered by sufferings of various kinds. The Council Fathers write, "Rather than be held back by perils and hardships in their apostolic labors they should rise to greater holiness, nourishing and fostering their action with an overflowing contemplation, for the delight of the entire Church of God."[8] In saying that priestly action is nourished and fostered with an overflowing contemplation, the Council is implying that the priest's ontological union with Christ, signified by the phrase "*in persona Christi*," also needs to be subjectively lived out; and this happens by way of prayer.

Vatican II's *Decree on the Training of Priests* (*Optatam Totius*) speaks about the priest's union with Christ in reference to the spiritual formation of seminarians. Here, the Council Fathers make the bold claim that the priest's union with God must be a continual reality:

> Spiritual formation should be closely associated with doctrinal and pastoral formation, and, with the assistance of the spiritual director in particular, should be conducted in such a way that the students *may learn to live in intimate and unceasing union with God the Father through his Son Jesus Christ, in the Holy Spirit.* Those who are to take on the likeness of Christ the priest by sacred ordination should form the habit of drawing close to him as friends in every detail of their lives.[9]

In saying that future priests are called to live "in intimate and unceasing union" with the Blessed Trinity, and that they are to "draw close" to Christ "as friends in every detail of their lives," the Council is saying again that the union with God being spoken of is not merely the union that is objectively rooted in Holy Orders, but is a union that is meant to be lived out subjectively and on a daily basis. There is nothing in the seminarian's life that should be excluded from friendship with Christ; everything in the seminarian is to be in communion with the Trinity.

The document makes clear that the pastoral ministry of the priest is not excluded from this intimate and unceasing union with Christ. Rather, the pastoral activity of the priest can be a means of spiritual growth: " . . . [Seminarians] . . . should . . . be trained to strengthen their spiritual life as fully as possible in the very exercise of their pastoral activity."[10] To use another expression, priests and seminarians are called to be "contemplatives even in action."[11]

Vatican II's *Decree on the Ministry and Life of Priests (Presbyterorum Ordinis)* is the document that speaks most of the priesthood. In writing this document, the Second Vatican Council wanted to "treat the subject of priests at greater length and with more depth"[12] than other documents had. In doing so, *Presbyterorum Ordinis* makes clear that the Sacrament of Holy Orders ontologically unites the priest to Christ, and that this union must be subjectively appropriated by the priest and intentionally lived out.

The ontological union of the priest with Christ is based upon the reality that the priest is configured to Christ the Head through the sacred character received at ordination. *Presybterorum Ordinis* states, "Through that sacrament priests by the anointing of the Holy Spirit are signed with a special character and so are configured to Christ the priest in such a way that they are able to act in the person of Christ the head."[13] The priest's sacramental union with Christ is so profound that it makes it possible for the priest to act "in the person of Christ the head" (*in persona Christi capitis*). It is important to note that this phrase is distinct from the simpler expression "*in persona Christi*" that was used in other Vatican II documents. According to Sr. Sara Butler, the use of this "more explicit expression" is a "genuine doctrinal development," insofar as the addition of the word "*capitis*" helps to "specify the essential difference" between the common and ministerial priesthoods.[14]

The subjective living out of this objective sacramental configuration and union with Christ is discussed in the third chapter of *Presbyterorum Ordinis,* entitled "The Life of Priests." Here, the Council exhorts priests to seek Christian perfection. The text specifies that " . . . priests are bound by a special reason to acquire this perfection." That special reason for the priest's call to perfection is that this perfection will help priests to be "living instruments of Christ the eternal priest."[15] To be an instrument of Christ necessitates living in communion with Christ—the priest, conscious of his human weakness, cannot be an instrument apart from Christ.

And yet, the Council says that the priest's human weakness is healed by Christ's own holiness: "The human weakness of his flesh is remedied by the holiness of him who became for us a high priest 'holy, innocent, undefiled, separated from sinners' (Heb. 7:26)."[16] The priest can take consolation from the fact that Jesus, the Divine Physician, who alone is holy, wants to be with the priest in that very place of weakness. As the Lord told St. Paul, "My grace is sufficient for you, for power is made perfect in weakness" (2 Cor. 12:9). The priest grows in holiness as he allows Christ to live in him, especially in areas of weakness.

This call to perfection or holiness in the life of the priest is important because although the sacraments work *ex opere operato*,[17] God Himself desires priests to be holy, and this holiness makes the priest's ministry more fruitful. In the words of *Presbyterorum Ordinis*:

> The very holiness of priests is of the greatest benefit for the fruitful fulfillment of their ministry. While it is possible for God's grace to carry out the work of salvation through unworthy ministers, yet God ordinarily prefers to show his wonders through those men who are more submissive to the impulse and guidance of the Holy Spirit and who, because of their *intimate union with Christ* and their holiness of life, are able to say with St. Paul: "It is no longer I who live, but Christ who lives in me" (Gal. 2:20).[18]

What does the priest's intimate union with Christ look like? The Council says that the priest's union with Christ involves letting Christ do all the work through him:

> By keeping in mind that it is the Lord who opens hearts and that the excellence comes not from themselves but from the power of God they will be more intimately united with Christ the Teacher and will be guided by his Spirit in the very act of teaching the Word. And by this close union with Christ they share in the charity of God, the mystery of which was kept hidden from all ages to be revealed in Christ.[19]

In other words, this union with Christ involves relying on God rather than on oneself. While a priest may be tempted to place too much emphasis on his own actions and gifts—which would move him in the direction of functionalism—the truth is that it is only "the Lord who opens hearts."[20] By living out of this recognition and relying on God to be at work in the hearts of those he serves, the priest is, then, more deeply united with Christ. It is also important to note that this text is saying that union with Christ—specified as "close union"—is meant to be experienced by the priest in the very midst of his ministry. Furthermore, this union also means that the priest will "share in the charity of God." To put it simply, the priest will have Christ's own Heart.

Sharing in the charity of God—having Christ's own Heart—can be summed up in the phrase "pastoral charity." Indeed, a very important aspect of communion with Christ in the life of the priest, which Vatican II highlights, is the fact that this communion is a communion with Christ's own pastoral charity. Pastoral charity translates into the priest being willing to lay down his life for the sheep as Christ did:

> While they govern and shepherd the People of God they are encouraged by the love of the Good Shepherd to give their lives for their sheep. They, too, are prepared for the supreme sacrifice, following the example of those priests who even in our own times have not shrunk from laying down their lives.[21]

It is important to note that it is the "love of the Good Shepherd" that encourages the priest to make this supreme gift of self. The priest cannot make this sacrifice with his own strength, but only in union with Christ.

While the Council is holding up martyrdom as the "supreme sacrifice," the Council also notes how even the praying of the Liturgy of the Hours and the administration of the Sacraments have a sacrificial dimension, as well. These sacrifices unite the priest with Christ's pastoral charity:

> In the same way they are united with the intention and the charity of Christ when they administer the sacraments. They do this in a special way when they show themselves to be always available to administer the sacrament of Penance whenever it is reasonably requested by the faithful. In reciting the Divine Office they lend their voice to the Church which perseveres in prayer in the name of the whole human race, in union with Christ who "always lives to make intercession for them" (Heb. 7:25).[22]

This availability of the priest for the celebration of the Sacraments, particularly the Sacrament of Penance, is part of the priest's need to have Christ's own Heart. The priest is called to host Christ's own availability.[23]

Communion with the pastoral charity of Christ helps lend inner unity to priests, who often feel scattered due to a sense of being pulled in many different directions. A passage of *Presbyterorum Ordinis* that Pope Benedict XVI also commented on in his essay *Life and Ministry of Priests* speaks of the inner division that can be present in the priest's life as a result of having so many external duties:

> In the world of today, with so many duties which people must undertake and the great variety of problems vexing them and very often demanding a speedy solution, there is often danger for those whose energies are divided by different activities. Priests who are perplexed and

distracted by the very many obligations of their position may be anxiously enquiring how they can reduce to unity their interior life their program of external activity.[24]

The problem is real. The multiplicity of a priest's activities—especially when pursued with a functional approach to the priesthood—can leave a priest feeling very fragmented. The solution to this inner disunity, according to the Council, is to seek union with Christ who does only the will of the Father:

> This unity of life cannot be brought about merely by an outward arrangement of the works of the ministry nor by the practice of spiritual exercises alone, though this may help to foster such unity. Priests can however achieve it by following in the fulfillment of their ministry the example of Christ the Lord, whose meat was to do the will of him who sent him that he might perfect his work.[25]

The Council is pointing to the fact that the priest may be tempted to think that by merely arranging his external activities in a more conducive way, or by practicing particular spiritual exercises, he will arrive at inner unity. On the contrary, the Council is saying that inner unity happens by the priest turning to the *Other* for help. Like Christ and with Christ, the priest will find inner unity by doing the will of the Father. The Council drives home this point by saying:

> The fact of the matter is that Christ, in order ceaselessly to do that same will of his Father in the world through the Church, is working through his ministers and therefore remains always the principle and source of the unity of their lives. Therefore priests will achieve

the unity of their lives by joining themselves with Christ in the recognition of the Father's will and in the gift of themselves to the flock entrusted to them. In this way, by adopting the role of the good shepherd they will find in the practice of pastoral charity itself the bond of priestly perfection which will reduce to unity their life and activity.[26]

Christ Himself, who works through His priests, is the source of unity for the priest. Christ in the priest does only the Father's will. Like Christ and with Christ, the priest is called to make a complete gift of himself to the flock. This communion with the pastoral charity of Christ means that the priest is a "good shepherd" living in union with "The Good Shepherd." This communion with Christ simplifies the priest's life and gives him a greater focus.

Seeking the Father's will in communion with Christ has some very concrete and practical ramifications. Namely, the priest is called to discern with Christ the will of the Father regarding each one of his activities:

To enable them to make their unity of life a concrete reality they should consider all their projects to find what is God's will—that is to say, how far their projects are in conformity with the standards of the Church's Gospel mission. Faithfulness to Christ cannot be separated from faithfulness to his Church. Hence pastoral charity demands that priests, if they are not to run in vain, should always work within the bond of union with the bishops and their fellow priests. If they act in this manner, priests will find unity of life in the unity of the Church's own mission. In this way they will be united with their Lord and through him with the Father in the Holy Spirit, and can be filled with consolation and exceedingly abound with joy.[27]

The priest needs to take stock of all his projects and activities and discern whether or not each one is the Father's will.[28] A good measurement of this is how much these activities are in accord with the bishop's vision and the mission of the Church. Union with the Trinity and obedience to the Church leads to an abundance of consolation wherein one overflows with joy.

Finally, the priest, living in communion with Christ the Good Shepherd, is called to share in Christ's own sacrifice to the Father. This happens primarily through the celebration of the Holy Eucharist, along with the maintenance of a deep life of prayer:

> Now this pastoral charity is derived chiefly from the Eucharistic sacrifice which is the center and source of the entire life of the priest, so that the priestly soul strives to make its own what is enacted on the altar of sacrifice. But this cannot be achieved except through priests themselves penetrating ever more intimately through prayer into the mystery of Christ.[29]

Therefore, it is essential for the priest to keep the Eucharist at the very center of his life. In fact, the Council "earnestly recommends" the daily celebration of Mass, "even if it is impossible for the faithful to be present."[30] Priests who offer daily Mass only when the faithful are present—that is, priests who offer the Mass only when they are scheduled to do so—could be inadvertently living out of a functionalist mentality insofar as they are offering the Mass more as a service to others than as something that is central to their own communion with Christ. As noble as it is for service to others to be the priest's goal, such service is fruitful only when it flows from the priest's communion with Christ's own pastoral charity, which is strengthened through the daily celebration of the Mass: "So when priests unite themselves with the act of Christ the Priest they daily offer themselves completely to God, and by being nourished with Christ's Body they share in the charity of him who gives himself as food to the faithful."[31]

NOTES

1. Second Vatican Council, "Decree on the Ministry and Life of Priests: Presbyterorum Ordinis," in *Vatican Council II: Vol. 1, The Conciliar and Post Conciliar Documents*, ed. Austin Flannery, new revised ed. (Northport, NY: Costello Publishing Company, 1998), sec. 2.

2. James Rafferty, Foreword to David Toups, *Reclaiming Our Priestly Character* (Omaha, NE: The Institute for Priestly Formation, 2010), xviii.

3. Second Vatican Council, "Dogmatic Constitution on the Church: Lumen Gentium," in *Vatican Council II: Vol. 1, The Conciliar and Post Conciliar Documents*, ed. Austin Flannery, new revised ed. (Northport, NY: Costello Publishing Company, 1998), sec. 10.

4. Samuel J. Aquila, "The Teaching of Vatican II on 'In Persona Christi' and 'In Nomine Ecclesiae'" in *Relation to the Ministerial Priesthood in Light of the Historical Development of the Formulae* (Rome: Pontificium Athenaeum Anselmianum, 1990), 1.

5. John Paul II, "Mystery and Worship of the Holy Eucharist," *Origins* 9, no. 41 (1980): 659.

6. Both the Council's text and John Paul II's explanation affirm the fact that the phrase *"in persona Christi"* refers to the ministerial priesthood and does not apply to the common priesthood of the faithful. For an in-depth discussion of this point, see Sara Butler, "Priestly Identity: 'Sacrament' of Christ the Head," *Worship* 70, no. 4 (July 1996): 290-306.

7. *Lumen Gentium*—due to the fact that it is a text that speaks primarily of the nature of the Church as a whole—does not speak of the ministerial priesthood in depth. While *Lumen Gentium* does not speak explicitly about the communion of the priest with Christ, the document does speak of "union" and "communion" with regard to the Church herself. See, for example, *Lumen Gentium*, secs. 3, 4, 7, 9.

8. *Lumen Gentium*, sec. 41.

9. Second Vatican Council, "Decree on the Training of Priests: Optatam Totius," in *Vatican Council II: Vol. 1, The Conciliar and Post Conciliar Documents*, ed. Austin Flannery, new revised ed. (Northport, NY: Costello Publishing Company, 1998), sec. 8. Emphasis added.

10. *Optatam Totius*, sec. 9.

11. Attributed to St. Ignatius of Loyola.

12. *Presbyterorum Ordinis*, sec. 1.

13. Ibid., sec. 2.

14. Butler, "Priestly Identity," 293. This specification is helpful, as there are a number of theologians who assert that all of the baptized can, in some sense, be considered as acting *"in persona Christi."* For example, regarding Holy Orders, Susan Wood writes that "there is a sense in which each baptized Christian can be understood to be configured to Christ and

to stand *in persona Christi*" (Susan Wood, "Priestly Identity: Sacrament of the Ecclesial Community," *Worship* 69, no. 2 [March 1995]: 112). Mark O'Keefe says something similar: "We could say broadly of every Christian that, by baptism into Christ and bearing his image, he or she represents Christ or is *alter Christus*, or acts *in persona Christi*. But only the ordained priest acts in the person of Christ as Head of his Body, the Church" (O'Keefe, 17). Nonetheless, Butler maintains that the Council actually "reserves the formula *in persona Christi* . . . for ministerial priesthood (Butler, 305)," but she says that "By adding 'capitis' to this expression [the Council] means to underline the distinction (Butler, 305)."

15.   *Presbyterorum Ordinis*, sec. 12.

16.   Ibid.

17.   *Catechism of the Catholic Church*, 2nd ed. (Washington, DC: USCCB, 2000), sec. 1128: "This is the meaning of the Church's affirmation that the sacraments act *ex opere operato* (literally: 'by the very fact of the action's being performed'), i.e. by virtue of the saving work of Christ, accomplished once for all. It follows that 'the sacrament is not wrought by the righteousness of either the celebrant or the recipient, but by the power of God.' From the moment that a sacrament is celebrated in accordance with the intention of the Church, the power of Christ and his Spirit acts in and through it, independent of the personal holiness of the minster. Nevertheless, the fruits of the sacraments also depend on the disposition of the one who receives them."

18.   *Presbyterorum Ordinis*, sec. 12. Emphasis added.

19.   Ibid., sec. 13.

20.   Ibid.

21.   Ibid.

22.   Ibid.

23.   What Deacon James Keating says of permanent deacons is true of priests who also retain the diaconal character: "He [the deacon] is the one who eagerly hosts the mystery of Christ's public service of charity *as his own*, as his new life." From James Keating, "The Character of Diaconal Ordination," *Ignatius Insight* (August 17, 2010), accessed May 21, 2015, http://www.ignatiusinsight.com/features2010/jkeating_diaconate_aug2010.asp.

24.   *Presbyterorum Ordinis*, sec. 14.

25.   Ibid.

26.   Ibid.

27.   Ibid.

28.   The priest would be aided in recognizing the Father's will through a proper discernment of spirits, such as that taught by St. Ignatius of Loyola. For a good treatment of Ignatian Discernment of Spirits, see Timothy M. Gallagher, *The Discernment of Spirits: An Ignatian Guide for Everyday Living* (New York: The Crossroad Publishing Company, 2005).

See also Timothy M. Gallagher, *Discerning the Will of God: An Ignatian Guide to Christian Decision Making* (New York: The Crossroad Publishing Company, 2009).

29. Ibid.
30. Ibid., sec. 13.
31. Ibid.

St. John Paul II
Communion with the Good Shepherd

In *Pastores Dabo Vobis*, St. John Paul II describes a fundamental concern in the priesthood today. He says that priests today are suffering from an "excessive loss of energy" that is caused by "ever-increasing pastoral activities."[1] He is not naming this issue as activism, *per se*; he is merely saying that the hard reality is that priests are simply very busy, and this busyness can be a source of exhaustion. These thoughts are echoed by Pope Francis, who stated in a homily for the annual Chrism Mass:

> The tiredness of priests! Do you know how often I think about this weariness which all of you experience? I think about it and I pray about it, often, especially when I am tired myself. I pray for you as you labour amid the people of God entrusted to your care, many of you in lonely and dangerous places. Our weariness, dear priests, is like incense which silently rises up to heaven (cf. *Ps* 141:2; *Rev* 8:3-4). Our weariness goes straight to the heart of the Father.[2]

The tiredness of priests results from the heavy labor of priestly ministry, and is something to be expected. When it is placed in relationship to the Father in communion with Christ, the heaviness is often lifted.

However, priestly weariness becomes a problem when it is compounded by activism—a cousin of functionalism—that John Paul II defines in *Pastores Dabo Vobis* as the reduction of ministry to the "provision of impersonal services," even if these services are of a "sacred" or "spiritual" nature.[3] The problem with activism is that it is "impersonal" and "businesslike."[4] When a priest falls into a mentality of activism or functionalism, the ministry is not undertaken in love; it is not Christ-like.

For John Paul II, much of the issue comes down to a crisis in priestly identity that arose in the years following the Second Vatican Council.[5] What is needed is a renewal in priestly identity—for the priest to understand that his identity is found in relationship with Jesus Christ.[6] Moreover, according to St. John Paul II, for a priest to be grounded in his identity in Jesus Christ, it is essential that he understand that the union with Jesus Christ that results from the Sacrament of Holy Orders needs to be lived out on a daily basis.[7] Ultimately, as Vatican II highlighted, the communion with Jesus Christ that a priest is called to live out is fundamentally a call to communion with Christ's own pastoral charity.[8]

The source of the priest's identity is found in the Blessed Trinity. St. John Paul II points to some profound words from the 1990 World Synod of Bishops[9] on the Trinitarian source of priestly identity:

> We derive our identity ultimately from the love of the Father, we turn our gaze to the Son, sent by the Father as high priest and good shepherd. Through the power of the Holy Spirit, we are united sacramentally to him in

the ministerial priesthood. Our priestly life and activity continue the life and activity of Christ himself. Here lies our identity, our true dignity, the source of our joy, the very basis of our life.[10]

Thus, the priest's joy is found not in fulfilling functions in a businesslike way; his joy is found in proclaiming the Father's love to the world by continuing Christ's activity through the union with Christ that happens via sacramental ordination.

St. John Paul II deepens this line of thought when he writes, "The priest finds the full truth of his identity in being a derivation, a specific participation in and continuation of Christ himself, the one high priest of the new and eternal covenant. The priest is a living and transparent image of Christ the priest."[11] When a priest realizes that he is "participating" in Christ's own life, indeed, "continuing" Christ's own life, and that he is a "transparent image"[12] of Christ, he understands the great dignity that is his and will be less tempted to give it all up when ministry becomes difficult.

Throughout *Pastores Dabo Vobis*, St. John Paul II speaks of the various effects of the Sacrament of Holy Orders. Summed up, St. John Paul II points to the union with Christ that happens via an ontological bond, a configuration to Christ as head and shepherd, a consecration to Christ, and the reception of pastoral charity.[13] He synthesizes these points in saying, "By the sacramental anointing of holy orders, the Holy Spirit configures them in a new and special way to Jesus Christ the head and shepherd; he forms and strengthens them with his pastoral charity . . ."[14]

In a reference to what is traditionally referred to as the "character" that is received in Holy Orders, but without using that specific word, St. John Paul II speaks of the "permanent" and "indelible" nature of what is received in the Sacrament:

> With the sacramental outpouring of the Holy Spirit who consecrates and sends forth, the priest is configured to the likeness of Jesus Christ, head and shepherd of the Church, and is sent forth to carry out a pastoral ministry. In this way the priest is marked permanently and indelibly in his inner being as a minister of Jesus and of the Church.[15]

This "mark" is something that happens in the "inner being" of the priest. This mark is very freeing for the priest, insofar as it "ensures that the priest can count on all the actual graces he needs, whenever they are necessary and useful for the worthy and perfect exercise of the ministry he has received."[16] For the priest to be able to "count on all the actual graces he needs" when carrying out his ministry means that he does not have to rely on himself but that he can and *must* rely on Christ.

It is not until later in the encyclical, when St. John Paul II is writing about the ongoing formation of priests, that he really fleshes out all that is received in the Sacrament of Holy Orders:

> The formation of the priest in its spiritual dimension is required by the new Gospel life to which he has been called in a specific way by the Holy Spirit, poured out in the sacrament of holy orders. The Spirit, by consecrating the priest and configuring him to Jesus Christ, head and shepherd, *creates a bond* which, located in the priest's very being, *demands to be assimilated and lived out in a personal,*

free and conscious way through an ever richer *communion of life* and love and an ever broader and more radical *sharing in the feelings and attitudes of Jesus Christ.* In this bond between the Lord Jesus and the priest, an ontological and psychological bond, a sacramental and moral bond, is the foundation and likewise the power for that "life according to the Spirit" and that "radicalism of the Gospel" to which every priest is called today and which is fostered by ongoing formation in its spiritual aspect.[17]

These words speak profoundly to the relationship between Holy Orders and communion with Christ. The Sacrament of Holy Orders, by way of the Holy Spirit, consecrates and configures the priest to Jesus Christ. A bond is formed with Christ in the very being of the priest. But this bond must be "assimilated and lived out." The living out of this bond is what St. John Paul II calls communion with Christ. He describes this communion as a "radical sharing in the feelings and attitudes of Jesus Christ."[18] The bond between Jesus and the priest is one that is ontological, psychological, sacramental, and moral. This bond is the foundation for the priest to live life in the Holy Spirit.

St. John Paul II speaks over and over of the centrality of communion with Christ in the life of the priest and how this communion with Christ needs to be lived out on a daily basis. For example, he speaks of "communion with God" as the "hinge" of the spiritual life of the priest:

Communion with God, which is the hinge on which the whole of the spiritual life turns, is the gift and fruit of the sacraments. At the same time it is a task and responsibility which the sacraments entrust to the freedom of the believer, so that one may live this same communion in the decisions, choices, attitudes and actions of daily existence.[19]

Here, it can be seen that communion with God is both a result of the Sacraments, as well as something that needs to be lived on a daily basis, in all that the priest does.

This communion with God—which St. John Paul II elsewhere describes as "intimate communion with the Blessed Trinity"[20]—is really a "novelty" for the believer and part of what makes a person a child of God. This "marvelous reality" is something that is "also at the heart of the spiritual life" and must be "radically renewed each day." This reality is well illustrated by Jesus Himself in the image of the vine and the branches, which St. John Paul II quotes substantially.[21]

While this mystery of communion with God is something that is meant for all Christians to experience, it is essential for the priest to experience this reality personally in order to communicate it to others: "Only if future priests, through a suitable spiritual formation, have become deeply aware and have increasingly experienced this 'mystery' will they be able to communicate this amazing and blessed message to others (cf. 1 Jn. 1:1-4)."[22] In the words of a familiar adage: "You can't give what you don't have." Priests must experience and live this amazing reality of communion with Jesus in order to help their fellow Christians come to live this mystery, as well. This communion is so central to the spiritual life that "it should . . . constitute the ethos of Christian living."[23]

The relationship between ordination and communion with Christ can be seen profoundly in words that St. John

Paul II spoke in a homily to five thousand priests from around the world:

> Beloved, through ordination, you have received the same Spirit of Christ, who makes you like him, so that you can act in his name and so that his very *mind and heart* might live in you. *This intimate communion with the Spirit of Christ*—while guaranteeing the efficacy of the sacramental actions which you perform *in persona Christi*—seeks to be expressed in fervent prayer, in integrity of life, in the pastoral charity of a ministry tirelessly spending itself for the salvation of the brethren. In a word, it calls for your personal sanctification.[24]

These words show that John Paul's thought is very much in accord with the Second Vatican Council's teaching that the objective dimension of communion with Christ that Holy Orders brings about—which makes the priest's own sacramental ministry efficacious—also needs to be subjectively appropriated by the priest in a personal way. This subjective appropriation of communion with Christ is part of the priest's "call to holiness."[25] And holiness is nothing short of "intimacy with God."[26]

As the priest heeds this call to holiness and begins living in this intimate communion with Christ, he simultaneously begins living in communion with Christ's own pastoral charity. St. John Paul II deepens this line of thinking that we saw articulated in the documents of the Second Vatican Council. According to St. John Paul II, pastoral charity can be described as "thinking and acting" like Jesus Christ, who is "head and shepherd of the Church."[27] Pastoral charity essentially involves a complete "gift of self"[28] for the flock that is the Church. It is due to this gift of self that one could say that pastoral charity counters functionalism, insofar as "It is not just what we *do*, but our gift of self, which manifests Christ's love for his flock."[29] In other words, the gift of self involves "being" rather than merely "doing," and in this way, pastoral charity goes against functionalism.

This communion with the pastoral charity of Christ needs to undergird every aspect of the priest's ministry. The priest finds that his activity "directs" him to seek out an "inner source," which is "the ever-deeper communion with the pastoral charity of Jesus." This communion, which is a result of "the outpouring of the Holy Spirit in the sacrament of orders," is the "principle and driving force of the priestly ministry."[30]

NOTES

1. John Paul II, *Pastores Dabo Vobis* (1992), sec. 3.
2. Francis, "Homily for Chrism Mass," April 2, 2015, accessed April 15, 2016, http://w2.vatican.va/content/francesco/en/homilies/2015/documents/papa-francesco_20150402_omelia-crisma.html.
3. *Pastores Dabo Vobis*, sec. 72.
4. Ibid.
5. Ibid., sec. 11.
6. Ibid., sec. 16.
7. Ibid., secs. 11, 25.
8. Ibid., sec. 57.
9. The subject of this synod, convened by John Paul II, was priestly formation in the circumstances of the present day. The encyclical *Pastores Dabo Vobis* was published two years after the conclusion of this synod.
10. *Pastores Dabo Vobis*, sec. 18.
11. Ibid., sec. 12.
12. In saying that the priest is a "living and transparent image of Christ the priest," John Paul II is also saying that the priest is at the "forefront" of the Church because he "represents" Christ (see *Pastores Dabo Vobis*, secs. 15, 16, 27). Therefore, it can be said that John Paul II follows a "representational" model of the priesthood rather than a functional model (for further explanation of these two models, see O'Keefe, *In Persona Christi*, 2.). Along these lines, while John Paul II says that "reference to the Church" is essential with regard to priestly identity—highlighting the importance of an "ecclesiology of communion" (*Pastores Dabo Vobis*, sec. 12)—the priest primarily represents Christ as head, shepherd, and spouse of the Church. See Butler, "Priestly Identity," for an in-depth discussion of the priest acting "*in persona Christi capitis.*"
13. *Pastores Dabo Vobis*, sec. 11.
14. Ibid., sec. 15.
15. Ibid., sec. 70.
16. Ibid.
17. Ibid., sec. 72. Emphasis added.
18. This truth that John Paul II highlights can be found in the writings of St. John Eudes (1601-1680), who wrote that "the Christian life must be a continuation of the most holy life which Jesus led on earth." Thus, "It necessarily follows that, just as the members are animated by the spirit of the head, and live the same life, so you must also be animated by the spirit of Jesus, live His life, walk in his ways, be clothed with His sentiments and inclinations, and perform all your actions in the dispositions and intentions that actuated His." From St. John Eudes, *The Life and the Kingdom*

of Jesus in Christian Souls: A Treatise on Christian Perfection for Use by Clergy or Laity (New York: P.J. Kennedy and Sons, 1946), 3.

19.   *Pastores Dabo Vobis*, sec. 48.

20.   Ibid., sec. 46. The rest of the quotes in this paragraph are also from sec. 46.

21.   It would be good to meditate upon these verses because of what the passage says about communion with Christ: "I am the true vine, and my Father is the vinedresser. . . . Abide in me, and I in you. As the branch cannot bear fruit by itself, unless it abides in the vine, neither can you, unless you abide in me. I am the vine, you are the branches. He who abides in me, and I in him, he it is that bears much fruit, for apart from me you can do nothing" (Jn. 15:1, 4-5, Revised Standard Version as quoted in *Pastores Dabo Vobis*).

22.   *Pastores Dabo Vobis*, sec. 46.

23.   Ibid.

24.   Ibid., sec. 33. Emphasis added.

25.   Ibid.

26.   Ibid.

27.   Ibid., sec. 21.

28.   Ibid., sec. 23. Emphasis added.

29.   Ibid.

30.   Ibid., 57.

Pope Benedict XVI
Going Deeper

Exploring the Word "Communion"

Pope Benedict XVI builds upon all that has been said by Blessed Columba Marmion, Vatican II, and St. John Paul II about communion with Christ as the antidote to functionalism in the diocesan priesthood. In particular, Benedict emphasizes even more strongly than the others how the Sacrament of Holy Orders unites the priest more closely to Christ and that this union is something that the priest must choose to live out each day. In his homilies and addresses to priests and seminarians, Pope Benedict speaks quite eloquently about how this communion with Christ must be at the heart of the priest's life and ministry. Benedict also helps us understand more fully what the word "communion" means and in doing so, he takes us into very deep theological waters.

A good place to begin looking at Benedict's formulation of the word "communion" is his work *Pilgrim Fellowship of Faith: The Church as Communion,* written before his election to the papacy. As the title of the book indicates, much of this work centers on communion with respect to the Church.

However, Joseph Ratzinger states over and over again that this communion with God comes before the communion of men with each other. The Church is founded on this communion with God in Christ. Ratzinger expresses it succinctly by saying, "To put it in the form of a concrete statement: the communion of people with one another is possible because of God, who unites us through Christ in the Holy Spirit so that communion becomes a community, a 'church' in the genuine sense of the word."[1]

Interestingly, Ratzinger teaches that the concept of communion of human beings with God is something that did not even exist in the Old Testament. The Hebrew word for communion is *chaburah*, and this word "is never used to designate the relationship between God and man; it is exclusively used to express relationships between men. There is no 'communion' between God and man; the Creator's transcendence remains insuperable."[2] It is only in and through Jesus Christ, as revealed in the New Testament, that communion of man with God is able to take place: "*the New Testament is this communion, in and through the person of Jesus Christ.*"[3]

In looking at the word "communion" in the New Testament, Ratzinger points to the description of the Church in Acts 2:42. In the Revised Standard Version of the Bible, this verse reads, "And they devoted themselves to the apostles' teaching and fellowship, to the breaking of bread and the prayers." Ratzinger notes that the word "fellowship" is κοινωνία (*koinonia*) in the Greek and *communicatio* in the Latin. Ratzinger asserts that in addition to fellowship and communion, the word *koinonia/communicatio* can also mean "Eucharist" or "congregation."[4]

While Ratzinger is speaking mostly about the communion or fellowship of the Church, he makes it clear that this "fellowship" is not merely a fellowship of human beings with one another but rather, it has its origin in Jesus Christ. As Ratzinger puts it, Jesus Christ is "the origin and heart of Christian communion."[5] As soon as a person is in fellowship with Jesus Christ, he or she can be in fellowship with other followers of Jesus.[6]

Another way of saying this is that the "vertical" dimension comes before the "horizontal." Commenting on the theologian Jerome Hamer, Ratzinger asserts, "Receiving comes before acting, or, as J. Hamer expresses it: In communion (κοινωνία) the horizontal dimension is the result of the vertical and can be understood at all only on that basis."[7] In other words, we can only be in communion with one another when we are first in communion with God.

Ratzinger makes the same point in an article in which he describes the origins of the *Communio* journal. Here, Ratzinger agrees with the theologian Oskar Saier, who says that Vatican II makes clear that the *communio* between believers flows from the *communio* that exists between God and man.[8] Ratzinger deepens the discussion by saying that " . . . we must remember that 'communion' between men and women is only possible when embraced by a third element."[9] What is this "third element"? It is, of course, God, who is both immanent and transcendent. It is worth quoting Ratzinger at length here in order to come to a deeper understanding of the word "communion," one that moves to the level of the mystical:

> Because both in its very depths and in its highest aspirations being a person goes beyond its own

boundaries towards a greater, universal "something" and even toward a greater, universal "someone." The all-embracing third, to which we return so often can only bind when it is greater and higher than individuals. On the other hand, the third is itself within each individual because it touches each one from within. Augustine once described this as "higher than my heights, more interior than I am to myself." This third, which in truth is the first, we call God. We touch ourselves in him. Through him and only through him, a *communio* which grasps our own depths comes into being.[10]

To put it another way, God—who is simultaneously beyond us and within us—is the one who brings about communion. This communion "grasps us" from within. Far from being an ethereal notion, communion with God is something that is found "in the historical reality of our lives."[11]

A discussion of the linguistic meaning of the word "*communio*" would be incomplete if it left out another possible meaning of the word: participation. Walter Cardinal Kasper, in his work *Theology and Church*, makes the point strongly that, in contrast to some who would like to reduce the word *communio* simply to "community," the word actually means "participation" in God. In Kasper's words:

> . . . the Greek word *koinonia* (Latin *communio*) does not originally mean community at all. It means participation, and more particularly, participation in the good things of salvation conferred by God: participation in the Holy Spirit, in new life, in love, in the Gospel, but above all, participation in the Eucharist.[12]

So according to Kasper, *communio* is primarily about participation in God. And this participation in God happens especially by way of the Eucharist. It is through the Eucharist that the Church is formed. Kasper makes this point by saying, "Augustine called the eucharist a 'sign of unity and a bond of love'. The last council took up this saying of Augustine's and based the communion of the church on the eucharistic communion."[13]

Like Kasper, Ratzinger shows how the word *communio* is translated as "participation" in one of St. Paul's Eucharistic texts:

> The cup of blessing which we bless, is it not a participation [κοινωνία; Vulgate, *communicatio*] in the blood of Christ? The bread which we break, is it not a participation [κοινωνία; Vulgate, *participatio*; Neo-Vulgate, *communicatio*] in the body of Christ? Because there is one bread, we who are many are one body, for we all partake of the one bread (1 Cor 10:16-17).[14]

In receiving the Body and Blood of Christ in the Holy Eucharist, the believer participates in Christ; he or she enters into communion with Christ. In becoming one with Christ, believers become one with each other; and the Church is, thus, formed. Ratzinger makes this point when he writes:

> Now the Whole attains its full concreteness; everyone eats the one bread and thus they themselves become one. "Receive what is yours," says Augustine, presupposing that through the sacraments human existence itself is joined to and transformed into communion with Christ. The Church is entirely herself only in the sacrament, i.e., wherever she hands herself over to him and wherever

he hands himself over to her creating her over and over again.[15]

Here, Ratzinger brings up a new aspect of communion with Christ: that communion with Christ involves a transformation. Communion involves not only a "joining" of two realities, but a transformation at the heart of one's existence: it is a transformation into communion with Christ.

This transformation into communion with Christ could also be described as "becoming" Christ, insofar as one can "become" the Eucharist. Ratzinger uses this language when he refers to one of St. Augustine's Easter homilies: "By eating the one bread, he comments, we ourselves become what we are eating." [16] Normally, when one eats food, the food becomes part of the person, but with the Eucharist, one becomes what one eats:

> Normal foodstuffs are less strong than man, they serve him: they are taken in so that they may be assimilated into man's body and build him up. This special food, however—the Eucharist—is, on the contrary, superior to man, is stronger than he is, and thus the process toward which the whole thing is directed is reversed: the man who takes this bread is assimilated to *it*, is taken into it, is fused into this bread and becomes like Christ himself. "Because the bread is one, we, the many, are one body."[17]

Simply put, what is happening in Eucharistic communion is actually an assimilation into Christ.[18] Thus, when a person fully enters into the Eucharistic mystery, a profound conversion takes place at the center of his being:

> The Eucharist is never an event involving just two, a dialogue between Christ and me. *Eucharistic communion* is

aimed at a complete reshaping of my own life. It *breaks up man's entire self and creates a new "we". Communion with Christ is necessarily also communication with all who belong to him: therein I myself become a part of the new bread that he is creating by the resubstantiation of the whole of earthly reality.*[19]

Ratzinger goes on to speak of communion with Christ as involving a "blending" into the "being of God." He uses this bold language when he says:

Jesus Christ, as we have acknowledged in our reflections thus far, opens the way to what is supposedly impossible, to the communion between God and man, because, as the incarnate Word, he is that communion. *In him we find the realization of that "alchemy" which transforms human existence and blends it into the being of God.* Receiving the Lord in the Eucharist, accordingly, means entering into a community of existence with Christ, entering into that state in which human existence is opened up to God and which is at the same time the necessary condition for the opening up of the inner being of men for one another. The path toward the communion of men with one another goes by way of communion with God.[20]

While the concept of a person becoming blended into the being of God might sound problematic theologically, it is important to note that Ratzinger is simply using striking language to speak about the reality of the union with God that takes place through the Eucharist. The fact that in the next sentence Ratzinger speaks of "entering into a community of existence with Christ" shows that Ratzinger is saying that even with this profound communion, the individual person will always remain distinct from Christ.[21]

In fact, the very word "communion" implies that two distinct realities—in our case, two distinct persons—are joined together while remaining individual entities. Ratzinger makes this clear, and brings us into an even deeper understanding of the word communion, by speaking of this word from a Christological perspective. Referring to the theological questions surrounding the Council of Chalcedon (451 A.D.) and the Third Council of Constantinople (680-681 A.D.), Ratzinger raises the question:

> What does "one Person in two natures" mean, for practical purposes, in real life? How can a person live with two wills and a dual intellect? And this is by no means just a matter of theoretical curiosity; this certainly also concerns us ourselves in the form of the question: How can we live as baptized Christians, as people of whom, according to Paul, it should be true that: "It is no longer I who live, but Christ who lives in me" (Gal 2:20)?[22]

This is really the heart of the question with regard to our own attempts to come to a deeper understanding of what "communion with Christ" really means. Communion with Christ, practically speaking, involves this bold statement of St. Paul, that "Yet I live, no longer I, but Christ lives in me" (Gal 2:20). But what does this mean?

Ratzinger points out that, with regard to the Christological question of how it is possible for Christ to have two natures in one Person, there were two solutions proposed in the seventh century. The first solution was to deny that Christ has an individual human will. This solution was rejected by the Third Council of Constantinople. The second solution was the opposite, that Christ had "two entirely separate spheres of willing."[23] The problem with this second solution is that "we end up with a kind of schizophrenia, with a conception that is as monstrous as it is unacceptable."[24] Ratzinger's summary of the Third Council of Constantinople's response to this solution shines light for us on what communion really means:

> The ontological *union* of two wills that remain independent within the unity of the person means, on the level of daily life, *communion* (κοινωνία) of the two wills. With this interpretation of the union as communion, the Council was devising an ontology of freedom. The two "wills" are united in that way in which one will and another can unite: in a common assent to a shared value. To put it another way: Both of these wills are united in the assent of the human will of Christ to the divine will of the Logos. Thus on a practical level—"existentially"— the two wills become one single will, and yet ontologically they remain two independent entities.[25]

So in the person of Jesus, the union of the two wills can, perhaps, better be described as a *communion* of the two wills, insofar as communion implies a certain freedom. The two wills in Christ assent to a shared value. In the same way, our human wills are free to follow God's will or not. As our human wills assent to the will of God in Christ Jesus, *communion with Christ* results. In other words, communion with Christ happens when we surrender our human wills to the Divine will.[26]

This surrender of our human wills to God's will involves some suffering on our part. Ratzinger calls it "the pain of this exchange."[27] Communion with God involves some pain because the assent of our will to God's will involves the death of the ego. It is this death that Jesus spoke of when He said, "Whoever wishes to come after me must deny himself, take up his cross, and follow me. For whoever wishes to save his life will lose it, but whoever loses his life for my sake and that of the gospel will save it" (Mk 8:34-35). While the Cross involves some pain, it is essential to embrace the Cross in order to be united with God. As Ratzinger says in *Jesus of Nazareth*, writing as Pope Benedict XVI, "The Cross . . . is the place of glory—the place of true contact and union with God, who is love . . ."[28]

Communion with Christ in the Priesthood

Having received a deeper understanding of the meaning of the word communion from Pope Benedict XVI, we are now in a better position to explore Benedict's thoughts on the role of communion with Christ in priestly life. This is best achieved by looking at various talks and homilies he gave as Pope, particularly on occasions connected to the priesthood. In doing so, we will see that Benedict not only builds on the thought of his predecessor St. John Paul II, but that he also brings us to even greater spiritual depths in his discussion of this subject.

Both the Second Vatican Council and St. John Paul II emphasized that the ontological union with Christ that comes about through the Sacrament of Holy Orders needs to be subjectively lived out in a priest's daily life. Pope Benedict XVI picks up this theme and emphasizes it, perhaps, even more strongly than Vatican II or John Paul II. This emphasis can be seen clearly in Benedict's homily for the Holy Thursday Chrism Mass in 2009:

Our being priests is simply a new and radical way of being united to Christ. In its substance, it has been bestowed on us forever in the sacrament. But this new seal imprinted upon our being can become for us a condemnation, if our lives do not develop by entering into the truth of the sacrament.[29]

What is made clear from Benedict's words is that while Baptism is the fundamental Sacrament that brings about union with Christ, the Sacrament of Holy Orders unites a man to Christ in a new and radical way. Yet, this radical union with Christ is not enough—the priest must enter into the truth of the Sacrament. If this personal appropriation of the Sacrament does not happen, the very seal of the character will become a "condemnation" for the priest. That is because the priest who is not in communion with Christ on a subjective level—even though he is objectively in union with Christ through the Sacraments—will not be living an authentic, integrated priestly life.

Pope Benedict makes the same point in an address he gave to priests of the Diocese of Rome in 2010. Here, he communicates to his priests that a call to the priesthood can only happen by way of a Divine initiative—it is only God who can "attract" a man to the priesthood.[30] In attracting a man to the priesthood, God gives him a great gift through the Sacrament of Ordination: "participation, communion with divine being, with the priesthood of Christ."[31] Yet, this gift of communion with the priesthood of Christ needs to be concretely lived out in a priest's life:

Let us also make this reality a practical factor in our life: if this is how it is, a priest must really be a man of God, he must *know God intimately* and know him in communion with Christ, and so we must *live this communion*; and the celebration of Holy Mass, the prayer of the Breviary, all our personal prayers are elements of being with God, of being men of God. Our being, our life, and our heart must *be fixed in God, in this point from which we must not stir.* This is achieved and reinforced day after day with short prayers in which we reconnect with God and become, increasingly, men of God who live in this communion and can thus speak of God and lead people to God.[32]

These words about the priest needing to know God intimately can perhaps stir up fear in a priest's heart. Some recent research has led to the conclusion that one of the greatest stresses that priests face is a type of "spiritual stress" due to the fact that priests "lack intimacy" with the One they "publicly represent."[33] However, Pope Benedict's words encourage us priests that we can, indeed, learn to be entirely "fixed in God, in this point from which we must not stir." This profound communion with Christ is not something that is meant for special mystics or for cloistered contemplatives as a reward for strenuous efforts at union with God. Rather, this communion is something that everyone, and particularly priests, as "men of God," can discover as something that flows from Holy Orders and is nourished by the ordinary life of prayer of a diocesan priest: the Holy Mass, the Breviary, and frequently reconnecting with God by way of short prayers voiced throughout the day.

In this way, Pope Benedict helps priests to discover the spiritual treasure that is found in the Sacrament of Holy Orders. During a homily for the ordination of priests, Benedict said, " . . . through the Sacrament [of Ordination] the priest is totally inserted into Christ, so that by starting from him and acting in his sight he may carry out in communion with him the service of Jesus, the one Shepherd, in whom God, as man, wants to be our shepherd."[34] The priest's communion with Christ flows from this total insertion into Christ and must be lived under God's gaze. This immersion in Christ means belonging entirely to God in a new way: "Priestly ordination means: being immersed in him, immersed in the Truth. I belong in a new way to him and thus to others, 'that his Kingdom may come.'"[35]

For a priest to be immersed in Christ and living in communion with Him means that the priest is no longer acting in isolation; he is no longer acting as if he were alone. As Benedict puts it, " . . . a priest is never alone because Jesus Christ is always with him."[36] This truth can help to dispel any sense of loneliness that a priest may experience, as John Paul II also noted.[37] However, in order to live this reality, there will necessarily be a certain suffering for the priest, insofar as he will have to die to his tendency toward independence rather than communion:

> In the words, "I do," spoken at our priestly ordination, we made this fundamental renunciation of our desire to be *independent*, "self-made." But day by day this great "yes" has to be lived out in the many little "yeses" and small sacrifices. This "yes" made up of tiny steps which together make up the great "yes" can be lived out without bitterness and self-pity only if Christ is truly the center of our lives. If we enter into true *closeness* to him.[38]

These words from Pope Benedict are very encouraging because he understands the difficulty involved in the sacrifices that priests have to make and the temptation toward self-pity. The priest's hope is found in closeness to Jesus and in allowing this whole mystery of communion with Christ to unfold gradually over time.

Pope Benedict often describes this communion with Christ simply as "being with" Christ. For example, in a homily given to seminarians and religious, Benedict speaks of how Jesus' call to the Twelve Apostles was, first and foremost, a call to "be with" Jesus:

> In his account of the call of the Twelve, [Mark] says: "Jesus appointed twelve to be with him and to be sent out" (3:14). To be with Jesus and, being sent, to go out to meet people—these two things belong together and together they are the heart of the vocation, of the priesthood. To be with him and to be sent out—the two are inseparable. Only one who is "with him" comes to know him and can truly proclaim him. And anyone who has been with him cannot keep to himself what he has found; instead, he has to pass it on."[39]

Simply put, "being with" Jesus is so essential in the life of the priest that if the priest is not *with* Christ, he will not *know* Christ and, thus, will not be able to make Him known to others. Once the priest knows Jesus through communion with Him, he cannot help but tell others about Him.

This "being with" Christ, this communion with the Lord, helps to dispel functionalism or activism in the priesthood. In making this claim, Benedict provides a helpful way of understanding the problem of activism in the priesthood:

> We know this from experience: whenever priests, because of their many duties, allot less and less time to being with

the Lord, they eventually lose, for all their often heroic activity, the inner strength that sustains them. Their activity ends up as an empty activism.[40]

Here, Benedict highlights one of the gravest deceptions to which a priest can fall prey: to believe the lie that his large amount of activity is "heroic" and, thus, very worthwhile. However, if the priest's activity is not done in communion with Christ—that is, if it is not sustained by prayer—it is completely empty.

Activism is dangerous and destructive because it can cause a priest to get off track. This is the point that Benedict makes in another Chrism Mass homily: "The priest above all must be a man of prayer. The world in its frenetic activism often loses its direction. Its action and capacities become destructive if they lack the power of prayer, from which flow the waters of life that irrigate the arid land."[41] Activism leads to a dry, hollow, empty, lifeless existence. Communion with Christ leads to an abundance of life and very fruitful and full activity in service of the Lord.

In fact, communion with Christ must undergird a priest's entire ministry. The call to "be with" or to "abide in" Jesus must be at the heart of everything a priest does:

We priests derive a particular vocation to pray in a strongly Christocentric sense: we are called, that is, to "remain" in Christ as the evangelist John likes to repeat (cf. Jn 1:35-39; 15:4-10) and this abiding in Christ is achieved through prayer. *Our ministry is totally tied to this "abiding"* which is equivalent to prayer, and draws from this its efficacy.[42]

To express it another way, abiding in Christ is not just something that would be *nice* for a priest to do in the course of his ministry. Rather, the priest's ministry is "totally tied to" remaining with Christ. Furthermore, as Christ himself tells us, a priest who does not remain with Him will be "thrown out like a branch and wither" (Jn 15:6). As Benedict says elsewhere, nothing that a priest does should be excluded from communion with Christ:

> [The priest] is a man of prayer, a man of forgiveness, a man who receives and celebrates the sacraments as acts of prayer and encounter with the Lord. He is a man of charity, lived and practiced, thus all the simple acts, conversation, encounter, everything that needs to be done, become spiritual acts in communion with Christ.[43]

Benedict is saying that this communion with Christ is not limited only to sacramental moments or to the particular times in which the priest acts *"in persona Christi."* Rather, the priest is called to be in communion with Jesus at all times—in his simple daily tasks, in the conversations he has with others, and so on.

When a priest lives in communion with Christ, he then becomes a bridge to God for others. In words that sound reminiscent of Blessed Columba Marmion, who spoke of being in "contact" with God,[44] Benedict voices in a General Audience talk that, "No man on his own, relying on his own power, can put another in touch with God. An essential part of the priest's grace is the gift, the task of creating this contact."[45] This gift the priest has for putting people in touch with God happens through the "being with Christ" that flows from the Sacrament of Holy Orders:

However, as an act of his infinite mercy, he calls some "to be" with him (cf. Mk 3:14) and to become, through the Sacrament of Orders, despite their human poverty, sharers in his own priesthood, ministers of sanctification, stewards of his mysteries, "bridges" to the encounter with him and of his mediation between God and man and between man and God (cf. *Presbyterorum Ordinis*, n. 5).[46]

It is important to note that the "human poverty" of the priest is all part of his acting as a bridge to God. God is merciful in calling men, who are conscious of our own weaknesses, to be bridges to God. The priest must not despair of his poverty and weakness, but rather see these as openings to God's merciful love and grace.

Having seen Pope Benedict XVI's great emphasis on the priest's absolute need for communion with Christ, a priest might then wonder *how* this communion with Christ might be cultivated. The simple answer is: prayer. For that reason, Benedict says that a priest "should make his spiritual life his highest priority."[47] This approach to the priesthood might initially strike the reader as surprising, since most diocesan priests may tend to think that our ministry should be our highest priority. However, communion with Christ—which has been shown to be the antidote to functionalism in the priesthood—only comes about through a very intentional and focused spiritual life. As Benedict puts it, "An intense spiritual life will enable him [the priest] to enter more deeply into communion with the Lord and to let himself be possessed by God's love, bearing witness to that love at all times, even in the darkest and most difficult."[48] Placing one's spiritual life as the highest priority is not opposed to the priest "remaining attuned to the concerns of his brothers and sisters."[49]

Pope Benedict XVI is able to make such a strong claim about the spiritual life being a priest's highest priority because, unlike a functionalist, Benedict is greatly concerned about the priest's personal growth. He would like to help priests find the inner unity that gives them joy in the midst of their many activities. In words that echo his "Life and Ministry of Priests," Benedict again proposes communion with Christ as this integrating factor: "To be able to grow, as persons and as priests, it is fundamental first of all to have intimate communion with Christ, whose food was to do the will of his Father (cf. Jn 4:34): all we do is done in communion with him, and we thus rediscover ever anew the unity of our lives in the many facets of our daily occupations."[50] Again, this communion with Christ comes about by making prayer a priest's highest priority. As Benedict puts it, "Thus, spending time in God's presence in prayer is a real pastoral priority; it is not an addition to pastoral work: being before the Lord is a pastoral priority and, in the final analysis, the most important."[51] This time in prayer is not meant to be "an additional burden that makes our day even more difficult."[52] Rather, the time in prayer is meant to be refreshing and a great help toward making a true gift of oneself.

Indeed, prayer must be so central in the life of the priest that the priest becomes a "master" of prayer. Benedict made this point in an address he gave to clergy in 2008. It would be helpful to quote him at length because he makes clear that he completely understands all of the obstacles priests face in making the time for prayer, and even gives personal examples in this regard:

Dear brother priests, if your faith is to be strong and vigorous, as you well know it must be nourished with assiduous prayer. Thus be models of prayer, become masters of prayer. May your days be marked by times of prayer, during which, after Jesus' example, you engage in a regenerating conversation with the Father. I know it is not easy to stay faithful to this daily appointment with the Lord, especially today when the pace of life is frenetic and worries absorb us more and more. Yet we must convince ourselves: the time he spends in prayer is the most important time in a priest's life, in which divine grace acts with greater effectiveness, making his ministry fruitful. The first service to render to the community is prayer. And therefore, time for prayer must be given a true priority in our life. I know that there are many urgent things: as regards myself, an audience, a document to study, a meeting or something else. But if we are not interiorly in communion with God we cannot even give anything to others. Therefore, God is the first priority. We must always reserve the time necessary to be in communion of prayer with our Lord.[53]

Pope Benedict is being very fatherly here to his priests, anticipating all of the objections that a priest might make as to why he cannot spend all the time he should in prayer: the frenetic pace of life, all of the worries, all of the talks and homilies that need to be prepared, and so on. For that reason, the priest must "convince himself" that prayer is more important than any of those things, for the communion with Christ that results from prayer is what enables the priest to have something to give to others.

Since Pope Benedict considers prayer as such a pastoral priority, and as the means for entering into the communion with Christ that is the antidote to functionalism in the priesthood, it would be helpful to explore the concrete suggestions that Benedict offers with regard to prayer in the life of the priest. We have already seen in the above quote how Benedict considers prayer to be a "regenerating conversation with the Father" and that it is important even to set prayer as a "daily appointment" in one's calendar. Pope Benedict is even more specific when he tells us elsewhere that this time in prayer should ideally be one hour in length. In recommending this timeframe, Benedict also gives some suggestions as to how the time should be spent: " . . . whatever the demands that arise, it is a real priority to find *every day an hour to be in silence with the Lord,* as the Church suggests we do with the breviary, with daily prayers, so as to return within the reach of the Holy Spirit's breath."[54] It is important to note here that the breviary could be part of this hour but should not be the entirety of the hour. Rather, there is a need for silence and the kind of prayer that puts one "within the reach of the Holy Spirit's breath." If the priest simply fills his entire time of prayer with the breviary, he is in danger of falling into functionalism—even in his prayer—in that he is simply continuing to accomplish his official tasks during the holy hour.[55]

Instead of letting one's daily holy hour become simply another area to fall into functionalism, Pope Benedict recommends that priests and seminarians see their time in prayer as time spent in "friendship with Jesus" and as a time to have a "heart-to-heart" conversation with Him.[56] The holy hour is a time in which a man's initial call to the priesthood can be renewed—that initial call which Benedict describes as a moment of "falling in love."[57]

Some final practical recommendations that Pope Benedict gives for prayer as a means to communion with Christ involve the importance of daily Mass with "deep interior participation," a heartfelt celebration of the Liturgy of the Hours, approaching the Sacred Scriptures as spiritual reading, and spending time in Eucharistic adoration.[58] When a priest allows his communion with Christ to grow through these means of prayer, he will have found the "treasure hidden in the field,"[59] and he will have boundless joy.

NOTES

1. Joseph Ratzinger, "*Communio:* A Program," *Communio* 19 (Fall, 1992): 444.

2. Joseph Ratzinger, *Pilgrim Fellowship of Faith: The Church as Communion* (San Francisco: Ignatius Press, 2005), 75.

3. Ibid. Emphasis in original.

4. Ratzinger, *Pilgrim*, 64.

5. Ibid., 65.

6. Ibid., 69.

7. Ibid., 72.

8. Ratzinger, "*Communio:* A Program," 443.

9. Ibid., 444.

10. Ibid.

11. Ibid.

12. Walter Kasper, *Theology and Church* (New York: Crossroads, 1989), 154.

13. Ibid.

14. Ratzinger, *Pilgrim*, 77.

15. Ratzinger, "*Communio:* A Program," 446-447.

16. Ratzinger, *Pilgrim*, 78.

17. Ibid.

18. St. Cyril of Alexandria spoke extensively about this Eucharistic fusion with Christ: "For 'he who eats my flesh', he says, 'and drinks my blood abides in me, and I in him.' For if someone were to fuse together two pieces of wax, he would no doubt be able to see that each had come to be in the other. In the same way, I think, anyone who receives the flesh of our Lord Jesus Christ and drinks his precious blood, as he himself says, comes to be one with him, mixed and mingled with him, as it were, through partaking of him, so that he comes to be in Christ, as Christ in turn is in him." From: Norman Russell, *Cyril of Alexandria: The Early Church Fathers*, ed. Carol Harrison (London: Routledge, 2000), 118, citing Cyril's homily Jo. 4.2.

19. Ratzinger, *Pilgrim*, 78. Emphasis in original.

20. Ibid., 79. Emphasis added.

21. In his article "The Fathers, the Scholastics, and Ourselves," *Communio* 24 (Summer 1997): 347-396, Hans Urs von Balthasar helps us to understand this paradox between union and distinction. He says, "This not-being-God of the creature must be maintained as the most fundamental fact of all, ranking first and above all others. That God is God: *This* is the most immense and absolutely *unsurpassable* thought. It says to me . . . that I myself . . . *am not God.*" (p. 354). It is this awareness of one's creaturehood that enables a person to enter into communion with the

Creator. Balthasar says, "Only where there is non-identity is love possible. And it is absolutely not true that love requires the abolition of personality, that it craves to be the Thou of the other. Even in the human sphere it wills rather the ever-greater exaltation and ecstasy of the beloved *simultaneously* with the greatest proximity and communion" (p. 355). The upshot of this paradox is that, "Even in the highest union, the individual ego does not experience annihilation but only the absorption [*Versinken*] of one's being *before* the overpowering greatness of the divine Being fulfilling me" (p. 359).

22. Ratzinger, *Pilgrim*, 80.

23. Ibid., 81.

24. Ibid.

25. Ibid.

26. For a wonderful description of surrender to God, see Wilfrid Stinissen, *Into Your Hands Father: Abandoning Ourselves to the God Who Loves Us* (San Francisco: Ignatius Press, 2011).

27. Ratzinger, *Pilgrim*, 82.

28. Benedict XVI, *Jesus of Nazareth: From the Baptism in the Jordan to the Transfiguration*, trans. Adrian J. Walker (New York: Doubleday, 2007), 73.

29. Benedict XVI, *The Priesthood, Spiritual Thoughts Series* (Washington, DC: United States Conference of Catholic Bishops, 2010), 10.

30. Benedict XVI, *The Priest: A Bridge to God* (Huntington, IN: Our Sunday Visitor, 2012), 52.

31. Ibid.

32. Benedict XVI, *Bridge*, 52. Emphasis added.

33. Gerard J. McGlone and Len Sperry, *The Inner Life of Priests* (Collegeville, MN: Liturgical Press, 2012), 3.

34. Benedict XVI, *Priesthood*, 7.

35. Ibid., 10.

36. Benedict XVI, *Bridge,* 59.

37. "Finally, it is in the context of the Church as communion and in the context of the presbyterate that we can best discuss the problem of priestly loneliness treated by the synod fathers. There is a loneliness which all priests experience and which is completely normal. But there is another loneliness which is the product of various difficulties and which in turn creates further difficulties. With regard to the latter, 'active participation in the diocesan presbyterate, regular contact with the bishop and with the other priests, mutual cooperation, common life or fraternal dealings between priests, as also friendship and good relations with the lay faithful who are active in parish life are very useful means to overcome the negative effects which the priest can sometimes experience' (quoting proposition 34 of the Synod)." John Paul II continues, "Loneliness does not however create only difficulties; it can also offer positive opportunities for the priestly life: 'When it is accepted in a spirit of oblation and is seen

as an opportunity for greater intimacy with Jesus Christ the Lord, solitude can be an opportunity for prayer and study, as also a help for sanctification and also for human growth.' (quoting proposition 35 of the Synod)" John Paul II, *Pastores Dabo Vobis*, sec. 74.

38. Benedict XVI, *Priesthood*, 27. Emphasis added.

39. Ibid., 45.

40. Benedict XVI, *Bridge*, 62.

41. Benedict XVI, *Priesthood*, 32.

42. Ibid. Emphasis added.

43. Ibid., 26.

44. Marmion, *Soul*, 416.

45. Benedict XVI, *Bridge*, 30.

46. Ibid.

47. Ibid., 34.

48. Benedict XVI, *Sacramentum Caritatis* (2007), sec. 80.

49. Ibid.

50. Benedict XVI, *Address to the Clergy of Rome* (May 13, 2005).

51. Ibid.

52. Ibid.

53. Benedict, *Bridge*, 50.

54. Ibid. Emphasis added. This recommendation of spending an hour each day in prayer is in harmony with Archbishop Fulton Sheen who is famous for his strong encouragement for priests to have a daily holy hour. His book *The Priest is Not His Own* (San Francisco: Ignatius Press, 2005) has a chapter on "Why to Make a Holy Hour?" and one on "How to Make the Holy Hour."

55. Fulton Sheen offers a concrete suggestion on this point: "Limit the saying of the breviary to twenty minutes of the hour . . . the Holy Hour is not an official prayer; it is personal. Each priest, being a man, has a heart unlike any other in the world. This unique heart must make up the content of his prayer. God no more likes "circular letters" than we do. In addition to liturgical or official prayer, there must be the prayer of the heart." Sheen, *The Priest is Not His Own*, 243.

56. Benedict XVI, *Priesthood*, 59.

57. Ibid., 61.

58. Benedict XVI, *Bridge*, 41.

59. Ibid. See Matthew 13:44.

St. John Mary Vianney
A Living Image of Communion with Christ

As Blessed Columba Marmion, the Second Vatican Council, St. John Paul II, and Pope Benedict XVI have all made clear, communion with Christ is not only possible, but essential, for the diocesan priest in the midst of a full and busy life of apostolic ministry. A perfect example of communion with Christ being lived in the midst of a very active diocesan priesthood can be found in the life of St. John Mary Vianney. This patron saint of priests is, perhaps, best known for his severe penitential practices and for the endless hours he spent hearing confessions. However, what is less known is that his apostolic zeal was the fruit of his deep, unceasing communion with Christ. John Vianney's profound communion with Christ can be seen in his own words, "Being a friend of God, being united to God . . . living in the presence of God, living for God. What a beautiful life! What a beautiful death! Everything before God's eyes; everything with God; everything for God's delight. What could make life more wonderful?"[1]

In a discussion of the malady of functionalism in the priesthood, St. John Vianney can be considered as a living, incarnate image of the antidote to functionalism—a living image of what communion with Christ "looks like" in the life of a diocesan priest. At first glance, it might seem unusual to speak of the Curé of Ars as a model for living in unceasing communion with Christ. Due to his enormous pastoral activity, some might consider him to be so active as to be thought of as a workaholic. One need only to look at his daily schedule to get a sense of just how active he was. We learn from Fr. George Rutler that the Curé's day began at 1:00 a.m. with prayer.[2] He heard the women's confessions until 6:00 a.m., at which point he celebrated Mass. From 6:00 a.m. to 8:00 a.m., he circulated among the pilgrims, speaking with them and blessing their medals. He would take half a cup of milk for breakfast, and then begin hearing the men's confessions until 8:30 a.m. At 10 a.m., he would take a break for prayers and then hear more confessions. He would pray the *Angelus* at noon and take his lunch while standing and speaking with visitors. According to Rutler, "The conversation during lunch was usually well animated, with the Curé telling most of the jokes."[3] At 12:30 p.m., he would go on sick calls. After Vespers and Compline, he would hear more of the women's confessions, followed by special evening conferences and a communal rosary. He finished his day somewhere between 10:00 p.m. and midnight. As Rutler sums it up, "This means he slept two hours at most before beginning a new day. And he did this seven days a week for thirty years."[4]

Today, we would be inclined to speak of such a schedule as a recipe for burnout. This is especially true when we learn that Vianney "never took a day off,"[5] nor did he go on retreat.[6] Moreover, he tried to make use of every spare moment, even during the few meals he took: "Still declining a chair during meals as a waste of time, since he liked to go through his mail while eating, he stood at a bare table in his bedroom."[7]

Even John Vianney's own words seem to condemn him as an activist. For example, Vianney once said, "If a priest should die from toiling for the glory of God and the salvation of souls, it would not be a bad thing."[8] Also, "The most common temptations are pride and impurity. One of the best ways of resisting them is a life of activity for the glory of God. Many people abandon themselves to a lax and idle life. No wonder the devil is able to put them beneath his feet."[9]

Was St. John Vianney an activist and a workaholic?[10] While the surface evidence seems to point to that possibility, a closer look at his interior life shows us that his was a life of deep communion with Christ. Everything he did, he did in union with Jesus. Activism is only activism when the activity is undertaken apart from Christ. When a lot of work is accomplished in communion with Christ, this is not activism or workaholism but, rather, a fruitful ministry that is accomplished according to the Father's will. In other words, what matters most is a person's interior disposition—not the amount of work or type of schedule he or she is living as viewed from an external perspective. Vianney's immense activity is not in any way in contradiction with his being in constant communion with Christ. Indeed, communion with Christ, rather than being something that is reserved to those living a less active, monastic or cloistered life, is something that is possible for highly active diocesan priests. In fact, it is this very communion with Christ that enabled the diocesan priest St. John Vianney to be as active and fruitful as he was.

It is abundantly clear from the evidence we have of his life that communion with Christ was at the very heart of St.

John Vianney's active priestly ministry. This truth is attested
to by Vianney's own words, and can be seen clearly in papal
writings about John Vianney over the last fifty years. To
gain a better understanding of the interior communion with
Christ that Vianney experienced, we will look at a few brief
examples from the writings of St. John XXIII, Blessed Pope
Paul VI, St. John Paul II, and Pope Benedict XVI.

St. John XXIII on St. John Vianney's Communion with Christ

The Curé of Ars himself spoke often of the need for
priests to seek a deep and intimate union with God. For
example, St. John XXIII, in his 1959 encyclical *Sacerdotii Nostri
Primordia*, quotes the Curé as saying, "The thing that keeps us
priests from gaining sanctity is thoughtlessness. It annoys us
to turn our minds away from external affairs; we don't know
what we really ought to do. What we need is deep reflection,
together with prayer and an *intimate union with God*."[11] Here,
Vianney really hits on the central issue: it is easier for the
priest to focus on the multiplicity of his external activities,
so much so that if he does turn his mind away from these
affairs, he does not even know what to do. But holiness is
found in seeking to live in an intimate communion with God.

John XXIII further illuminates this reality in saying,
regarding Vianney, that "The testimony of his life makes it
clear that he always remained devoted to his prayers and that
not even the duty of hearing confessions or any other pastoral office could cause him to neglect them. 'Even in the midst
of tremendous labors, he never let up on his conversation
with God.'"[12] This latter point is really the secret of sanctity
and what communion with Christ is all about: it is constant
conversation with God in the midst of great apostolic labor.

This is the way that Jesus Himself lived, in constant communication with the Father: "Truly, truly I say to you, the Son can do nothing of his own accord, but only what he sees the Father doing . . . " (Jn 5:19).

Union with God is the sole source of a priest's happiness. It is not his ministry that satisfies him; it is only God who satisfies. As the Holy Curé puts it, "Man is so great that nothing on earth can satisfy him. He can only be happy when he turns to God. . . . Take a fish out of water, and it will cease to live. There you have it: the same thing happens to a man without God."[13] Indeed, more than a matter of happiness versus sadness, turning to God is a matter of life versus death. Many priests, not living united to God, and living purely exterior rather than interior lives, are spiritually dead, like fish out of water.

A fish cannot survive outside of water. Neither can man survive without breathing. And so Vianney wisely remarks, "We should never interrupt God's presence, just as we never interrupt our breathing."[14] Physical breathing keeps us physically alive; spiritual breathing by living in God's presence keeps us spiritually alive. Pope Benedict XVI said something similar when he stated that spending time with God is what provides "space for the soul to draw breath, without which we necessarily become breathless—we lose that spiritual breath, the breath of the Holy Spirit within us."[15]

It is easy for us priests to fall into the trap of thinking that our work is so important that nothing, not even prayer, should take us away from it. To that erroneous thinking, Vianney replies, "As important as our work may be, we can always pray without harming our affairs."[16] Vianney's words are quite an understatement: praying not only does not harm our affairs but rather, makes our affairs fruitful and leads us into deep personal holiness. Without prayer, there is no priestly holiness. This truth can be seen when Vianney says, amplifying what he said previously, that "What keeps us priests away from holiness is a lack of reflection. We do not return back to ourselves; we do not know what we have done. What we need is reflection, prayer, and *communion with God.*"[17]

It is necessary for the priest to "return back to himself," back to interiority, in order to have this communion with God. John Vianney deeply laments this lack of interiority among priests when he says, "What a disgrace for a priest not to have an inner life! . . . But calm, silence, and concentration are necessary in order to have one." It is sometimes difficult for priests to find this calm, silence, and concentration, but Vianney reminds us that "It is in silence that God speaks."[18]

Blessed Pope Paul VI on St. John Vianney's Communion with Christ

In the same year that St. John XXIII's encyclical on the priesthood was published (1959), Cardinal Giovanni Battista Montini, Archbishop of Milan, later to be Pope Paul VI, gave a speech at the conclusion of a small diocesan synod, in which he spoke about St. John Vianney. In a text transcribed from his speech, Blessed Paul VI gives an excellent description of functionalism, giving concrete, helpful examples:

> The first temptation is to limit our ministry to the search for means. You might say the following: "I am going to build a small chapel, I have to build the church, I have to pay the debts, I need to publish a book, and I have to set up a school." These are all means. However, if I limit my priestly activities to the search for and attainment of means, and make this the measure of my success—oh!

what a good priest: he built a house, there was no rectory and he built one, there was no soccer field and he was able to make one, he put a movie projector in his parish, and so forth, which I repeat are all means that we should certainly be concerned with—and if my plan for priestly accomplishment remains only this, then I am a priest who has understood neither our time, nor the example of the Curé of Ars, nor the mystery of Christ working through me.[19]

Paul VI's description of priestly temptation in 1959 is just as true—perhaps, even more so—today. Priests today are very much tempted to measure themselves based on their external accomplishments. A "good priest" is seen as one who builds edifices, balances the budget, publishes books, and so on. But these external activities are not what priesthood is all about. Rather, priesthood is about communion with Christ:

And here again the life of the Curé of Ars provides us with images that speak volumes, and they speak so loudly that they take our voice away and leave us silent. In other words, a man who lives his priesthood in this manner will enter into an *experience of Christ himself* not just in terms of an *external imitation*, but in terms of a certain shared life in the present moment, a *self-aware reproduction of Christ* in his own person.[20]

Priesthood, in other words, is truly priesthood when the priest participates and shares in Christ's own life, experiencing Him and not merely imitating Him externally, and allowing Christ to be reproduced in the priest's own person. That is a much different focus than having one's mind set on simply updating the parish facilities with the latest technology.

St. John Paul II on St. John Vianney's Communion with Christ

In 1986, on the bicentennial of the birthday of the Curé of Ars, St. John Paul II focused his Holy Thursday letter to priests on St. John Vianney as a model for priestly living. John Paul, aware of the many struggles that priests face today, wrote in his letter, "While recognizing a unique grace granted to the Curé of Ars, do we not find here the sign of hope for today's priests who are suffering in a certain spiritual desert?"[21]

While St. John Paul II cites many reasons as to why the Curé is such a wonderful model for priests, I would like to specifically highlight what John Paul II says about Vianney's communion with Christ. In particular, John Paul II emphasizes how central prayer was in the life of the Curé:

> Prayer was the soul of his life: silent, contemplative prayer, usually at the foot of the tabernacle in his church. Through Christ, his soul was opened to the Three Divine Persons to whom he would consign "his poor soul" in his last will and testament. "He maintained constant union with God in the midst of his very busy life." And he neglected neither the Divine Office nor the Rosary. He would spontaneously turn to the Virgin.[22]

For John Vianney, prayer was everything; it was "the soul of his life." He lived in intimate and unceasing communion with the Blessed Trinity in the midst of his very active ministry. His life of prayer was so intimate and so real that he once said, "Prayer is like two friends living together."[23]

St. John Paul II highlights how the Curé's union with God was the key to drawing others into deeper intimacy with God. In explaining this dynamic, the Pope makes the distinction between the objective and subjective dimension of the Sacraments, but shows how both are necessary:

> John Mary Vianney definitively sanctified himself in order to better sanctify others. Of course, conversion remains a secret of the heart, free to make its decision, and a secret of God's grace. With his ministry, a priest can only enlighten the person, guide him to the confessional, and give him the sacraments. These sacraments are indeed acts of Christ, and their efficacy is not diminished by the imperfection or unworthiness of the minister. *But the result also depends on the disposition of the recipient, and that disposition is powerfully aided by the personal holiness of the priest,* by his proven witness, and also by the mysterious exchange of merits in the Communion of Saints.[24]

In other words, a priest's communion with Christ somehow, mysteriously and mystically, very much helps the recipients of the Sacraments to grow in holiness. For St. John Vianney, his communion with Christ drew others into this same communion in such a tangible way that George Rutler remarked, "The sermons of these last days had become almost entirely public conversation with the Blessed Sacrament."[25] In fact, as St. John Paul II tells us, the Curé would often point to the tabernacle in the middle of his homilies and say, "He is there!"[26]

In addition to referencing Vianney in a Holy Thursday letter written in 1986, St. John Paul II again pointed to the Curé of Ars in a retreat that he gave in Ars that same year for priests, deacons, and seminarians. On this retreat, John Paul II underscored how priesthood is about *being* rather than *doing*; in other words, who priests *are* is more important than what they *do*:

It [priesthood] is not merely a task that we have received or a qualified function to be carried out in service of the People of God. Some may speak of the priesthood as a job or a function, including the function of presiding over the eucharistic banquet. *But we cannot be reduced to being its functionaries.* This is first of all because it is within our very being that we are signed through ordination with a unique character that configures us to Christ the Priest in order to make us capable of acting in the name of Christ the Head in person.[27]

When a priest is tempted to think of his priesthood as merely a job or function, he need only remember that he has been marked with the sacerdotal character through the Sacrament of Holy Orders, and then seek to live in communion with the One to whom he has been configured.[28]

When priests are living in communion with Christ, they will know who they truly are, and will be set free from merely going through the motions of ministry on a surface level. According to St. John Paul II, St. John Vianney is a priest who lived on a deeper level: "It is precisely in the Curé of Ars that we see a priest who was not content to merely go through the external motions of the redemption; he participated in it with his very being, in his love of Christ, in constant prayer, in the offering of his trials and voluntary mortifications."[29] St. John Vianney himself reveals his awareness of who he is when he says, "It is priests who continue the work of redemption on earth."[30]

If there is any doubt about how important union with God was in the life of St. John Vianney, one need only look at how often he spoke of the word "salvation." According to St. John Paul II, "salvation" and "union with God" are so closely related that they are the same reality:

> The word "salvation" was frequently on the lips of the Curé of Ars. What did it mean for him? Being saved means being freed from sin, which distances us from God, hardens our hearts, and risks separating us from God's love forever, which is the most atrocious fate. *Being saved is living united to God*; it is seeing God.[31]

In other words, salvation is not only something that occurs at the end of a person's life on earth. Rather, salvation is a reality that is meant to be experienced here and now as a person is freed from sin and begins to live in a closer union with God. This movement of letting go of sin and living in deeper union with God involves a person coming to see that real joy is found not in sin but in intimacy with God. Fr. Frederick Miller puts it beautifully, "It is a great grace for the sinner to experience interiorly that the pleasure of union with God is far better than the gratification afforded by any sin."[32]

Salvation involves a "spiritual renewal," as well, and is something that priests must enter into before they can help others along this journey of union with God. In St. John Paul II's words to his retreatants:

> You, too, will therefore know the journey of salvation and the means for restoring yourselves. I would first of all say this: a spiritual renewal. How can we bring an end to the spiritual crisis of our time if we ourselves do not take advantage of that *profound and constant union with the Lord* that we are here to serve? We find an unparalleled guide in the Curé of Ars. He said that "a priest is first and foremost a *man of prayer* . . . the *intimate union* that we need with God is meditation and prayer."[33]

These are strong words from St. John Paul II. That we, priests, live in a profound, intimate, and constant union with Christ is essential in order to emerge from our current spiritual crisis. The priest—according to Vianney—must, therefore, be "first and foremost a man of prayer."

When a priest lives in this intimacy with God, the priesthood itself becomes a vehicle for his own growth in holiness. As John Paul II puts it, "the priestly ministry therefore becomes the daily grounds for our sanctification when lived in a *state of union with God*."[34] It is important to note that the Pope refers to union with God as a "state" that a priest may live in. Again, John Paul is not speaking of the objective union with God that flows from the sacraments, but is speaking about the subjective living out of this union with God on a daily basis. For St. John Vianney, this state of union with God meant that no part of himself was separated from God in any way: "Belonging to God, being entirely God's with no separation, the body of God, the soul of God, a chaste body, and pure soul: there is nothing more beautiful!"[35]

Pope Benedict XVI on St. John Vianney's Communion with Christ

When Pope Benedict XVI, in 2009, announced a special Year for Priests, he did so in conjunction with the 150th anniversary of the death of St. John Vianney. The Pope called for this Year for Priests in order to "encourage priests in this striving for spiritual perfection on which, above all, the effectiveness of their ministry depends."[36] Benedict, like his predecessor, draws attention to the fact that priestly holiness is not a secondary concern, but directly impacts the effectiveness of the priestly ministry. In stressing this truth, Benedict points to the Curé of Ars as "a true example of a pastor at the service of Christ's flock."[37]

One of the essential elements of the priestly ministry that Pope Benedict underlines is the "communal" dimension. While this communal aspect refers to communion with other people, the communion is grounded primarily in intimacy with God:

> The mission is "communal" because it is carried out in a unity and communion that only secondly has also important aspects of social visibility. Moreover, these derive essentially from that *divine intimacy* in which the priest is called to be expert, so that he may be able to lead the souls entrusted to him humbly and trustingly to the same encounter with the Lord.[38]

These words about the priest needing to be an expert in divine intimacy hearken back to what Pope Benedict said in an address to the clergy of Warsaw in 2006: "The faithful expect only one thing from priests: that they be specialists in promoting the encounter between man and God. The priest is not asked to be an expert in economics, construction or politics. He is expected to be an expert in the spiritual life."[39] The people, in other words, look to the priest in order to find God: "God is the only treasure which ultimately people desire to find in a priest."[40]

We learn from St. John Vianney that the communion with Christ that the priest is invited into can be seen particularly as a union with Christ's own heart. Pope Benedict made this clear in a homily he gave on the Solemnity of the Sacred Heart of Jesus in 2009—the first day of the Year for Priests. The Pope pointed out how the Sacred Heart of Jesus, far from simply being merely a pious devotion, is actually at the very center of the Christian life: "The very core of Christianity is expressed in the heart of Jesus."[41]

The heart of Jesus is so central to Christianity because Jesus desires that His followers "abide" in His love, and His love is expressed in His heart. This abiding with Jesus, which is meant for all of His disciples, is particularly important for priests, as Benedict XVI points out:

> While it is true that Jesus' invitation to "abide in my love" (cf. Jn 15:9) is addressed to all the baptized, on this feast of the Sacred Heart of Jesus, the day of prayer for the sanctification of priests, this invitation resounds all the more powerfully for us priests. It does so in a special way this evening, at the solemn inauguration of the Year for Priests which I have proclaimed to mark the 150th anniversary of the death of the saintly Curé of Ars.[42]

Benedict goes on to quote the famous definition of the priesthood that was given by the Holy Curé:

> A lovely and touching saying of his, quoted in the *Catechism of the Catholic Church,* comes immediately to mind: "the priesthood is the love of the heart of Jesus" (n. 1589). How can we fail to be moved when we recall that the gift of our priestly ministry flows directly from this heart? How can we forget that we priests were consecrated to serve, humbly yet authoritatively, the common priesthood of the faithful? Ours is an mission [*sic*] which is indispensable for the Church and for the world, a mission which calls for complete fidelity to Christ and *constant union* with him. To abide in his love entails constantly striving for holiness, as did Saint John Mary Vianney.[43]

This constant union with Christ means that the priest will actually have the same heart as Christ—in other words, the priest will be united to Christ's own heart. When a person encounters the priest, that person will encounter the very heart of Christ. St. John Vianney is a living image of this reality. As Raymond Cardinal Burke puts it, "As the Curé of Ars understood so well, the priest finds his *identity* in the Heart of Jesus the high priest."[44]

This union with the heart of Jesus involves a larger plan: that Christ would actually become the very "heart of the world." Pope Benedict uses these profound words when he says:

> Only in this way can we cooperate effectively in the mysterious "plan of the Father" which consists in "making Christ the heart of the world"! This plan is accomplished in history as Jesus gradually becomes the Heart of human hearts, beginning with those called to be closest to him: namely his priests.[45]

Here again, the Pope underscores the fact that the starting point for Christ becoming the heart of the world is for priests to be the first to allow Jesus to be the Heart of their own hearts. When we priests allow Christ to be the center of our hearts, then Christ can reign more fully in every human heart.

Priests must not despair when they see this lofty call to union with the heart of Jesus and simultaneously, see their own weaknesses. It is our very weaknesses that draw us close to Christ's own heart. As Pope Benedict puts it, "Even our shortcomings, our limitations and our weaknesses ought to bring us back to the heart of Jesus."[46] Pope Francis similarly told us on a more recent Solemnity of the Sacred Heart, "Let us be not afraid to approach him! He has a merciful heart!"[47]

As priests are drawn into the heart of Jesus and united with His heart, we are united to Christ's own pastoral charity, which flows from the heart of Jesus. Pope Benedict makes this clear toward the end of his homily on the Solemnity of the Sacred Heart of Jesus in 2009, when he speaks of his experience of venerating the relic of St. John Vianney's heart:

> A few moments ago, in the Choir Chapel, I was able to venerate the relic of the saintly Curé of Ars: his heart. A heart that blazed with divine love, experienced amazement at the thought of the dignity of the priest, and spoke to the faithful in touching and sublime tones, telling them that "after God, the priest is everything! . . . Only in heaven will he fully realize what he is."[48]

The heart of the Curé of Ars was a heart ablaze with Divine love—in other words, filled with pastoral charity. Indeed, Frederick Miller points out that we learn from St. John Vianney that a priest should not be surprised to discover an abundance of pastoral charity already in his heart because this charity is rooted in Holy Orders:

> If the character of holy orders is indeed the charism of Jesus, the Good Shepherd, it is supernaturally natural for the priest to discover deep springs of pastoral charity in his heart. This supernatural instinct impelled John Vianney to go and seek out his people when he took up his post in Ars.[49]

Pope Benedict XVI exhorts his priests to pray for this gift of pastoral charity that leads to a total gift of self: "In the

Eucharistic Adoration which is to follow our celebration of Vespers, let us ask the Lord to set the heart of every priest afire with that 'pastoral charity' which can make him one in heart and mind with Jesus the High Priest, and thus to imitate Jesus in complete self-giving."[50]

NOTES

1.   Leonardo Sapienza, ed., *Reflections on Priestly Life: In the Footsteps of St. John Vianney, the Curé of Ars* (Washington, DC: United States Conference of Catholic Bishops, 2011), 44.

2.   George William Rutler, *The Curé D'Ars Today* (San Francisco: Ignatius, 1988), 187-189.

3.   Ibid., 188.

4.   Ibid.

5.   Ibid., 189.

6.   Ibid. This is because "the bishop, possibly with imprudence, insisted that a retreat would be superfluous."

7.   Rutler, *Curé D'Ars*, 218-219.

8.   Sapienza, *Reflections on Priestly Life*, 69.

9.   Ibid., 77.

10.   Some would accuse St. John Vianney of being not only a workaholic, but a "madman" due to his austere way of life and intense activity. George Rutler answers this objection: "A madman may be mad about just one thing, or about many things, but not about everything: either Vianney was beyond madness or he was totally sane. Certainly there was no evidence of dysfunctional anxiety . . . the Curé's personality was not unhinged . . . he was in the admittedly suspicious role, but in his case a perfectly true role, of being the only man on parade who was not out of step." From Rutler, *Curé D'Ars*, 170. The problem is that "When grace is denied, the only explanation for it is insanity" (Rutler, 211). The truth is that "holiness can make a man whole" (Rutler, 212).

11.   John XXIII, *Sacerdotii Nostri Primordia* (1959), sec. 37, accessed October 23, 2015, http://w2.vatican.va/content/john-xxiii/en/encyclicals/documents/hf_j-xxiii_enc_19590801_sacerdotii.html. Emphasis added. This encyclical speaks of certain aspects of priestly life and was written in 1959, which was the centennial of St. John Vianney's death, as well as the fifty-fifth anniversary of John XXIII's priestly ordination.

12.   Sapienza, *Reflections on Priestly Life*, 15, citing *Sacerdotii Nostri Primordia*, sec. 37.

13.   Ibid., 44.

14.   Ibid., 46. According to George Rutler, a parallel can be seen here between St. John Vianney and a Russian contemporary of his, Fr. John of Kronstadt (1829-1908) who lived a life of great austerity and heard close to three hundred confessions daily. Like Vianney, remaining in the presence of God was everything to him. According to Rutler, he "lived the divine liturgy as heaven on earth," and once exclaimed, "Oh my Lord Jesus Christ! Thou art all present! We see, touch, perceive, and feel thee here! The highest recompense for a Christian, especially a priest, is the

presence of God in his heart. His is our life, our glory." See Rutler, *Curé D'Ars*, 208-209.

15.   Ratzinger, *Pilgrim Fellowship of Faith*, 171.

16.   Sapienza, *Reflections on Priestly Life*, 46.

17.   Ibid., 48. Emphasis added.

18.   Ibid., 48.

19.   Ibid., 62.

20.   Ibid. Emphasis added.

21.   Ibid., 82.

22.   Ibid., 88.

23.   Rutler, *Curé D'Ars*, 147.

24.   Sapienza, *Reflections on Priestly Life*, 89. Emphasis added.

25.   Rutler, *Curé D'Ars*, 219.

26.   Sapienza, *Reflections on Priestly Life*, 85.

27.   Ibid., 96. Emphasis added.

28.   Frederick Miller further elucidates this reality when he says, "First, the apostles were chosen to share in Christ's life and mission, to be his envoys. They must *be* with him, and only then will they be sent out. Priestly ontology both precedes and governs priestly function. In other words, the apostles, through spiritual intimacy with Christ, would be given the capacity to do the things that he did. This transformation means nothing less than an abiding and real presence of Christ in his apostles." Frederick Miller, *The Grace of Ars* (San Francisco: Ignatius, 2010), 13.

29.   Sapienza, *Reflections on Priestly Life*, 97.

30.   Ibid., 95. The full quote from St. John Paul II is, "St. John Vianney even said, 'Without priests, the Passion and death of our Lord would be for nothing. It is priests who continue the work of redemption on earth.'"

31.   Ibid., 101-102. Emphasis added.

32.   Miller, *The Grace of Ars*, 87.

33.   Sapienza, *Reflections on Priestly Life*, 109-110. Emphasis added.

34.   Ibid., 111. Emphasis added.

35.   Ibid., 76.

36.   Ibid., 127.

37.   Ibid.

38.   Ibid., 128.

39.   Benedict XVI, "Address by the Holy Father: Meeting with the Clergy," Warsaw Cathedral, May 25, 2006, accessed April 15, 2015, http://w2.vatican.va/content/benedict-xvi/en/speeches/2006/may/documents/hf_ben-xvi_spe_20060525_poland-clergy.html.

40.   Sapienza, *Reflections on Priestly Life*, 128, quoting Benedict XVI.

41.   Benedict XVI, "Homily of His Holiness Benedict XVI: Opening of the Year for Priests on the 150th Anniversary of the Death of Saint John Mary Vianney," June 16, 2009, St. Peter's Basilica, accessed November 18, 2014, http://www.

vatican.va/holy_father/benedict_xvi/homilies/2009/documents/
hf_ben-xvi_hom_20090619_anno-sac_en.html.

  42. Ibid.

  43. Ibid. Emphasis added.

  44. Raymond Burke, "Foreword," in Miller, *The Grace of Ars*, x.

  45. Benedict XVI, "Opening of the Year for Priests."

  46. Ibid.

  47. Francis, "Sunday Angelus," (June 9, 2013), accessed April 15, 2015, http://en.radiovaticana.va/storico/2013/06/09/
pope_francis_sunday_angelus_(full_text)/en1-699870.

  48. Benedict XVI, "Opening of the Year for Priests."

  49. Miller, *Grace of Ars*, 4.

  50. Benedict XVI, "Opening of the Year for Priests."

Living in Communion with Christ

This book began by highlighting functionalism as a disease that is afflicting the contemporary diocesan priesthood. Functionalism, as it pertains to the priesthood, has been described as an approach to life wherein a priest derives his identity from his activity, his work, his success, his titles, his rewards, his achievements, his fidelity to his duties, and so on. In other words, in a functionalist mentality, the priest places his activity or "mission" first, before his relationship with God. Such an approach to the priesthood results in a faulted notion of priestly identity and a sense of emptiness in a priest's life—an emptiness that is often filled with frenetic activity or with behaviors that are not consonant with who the priest is as a man of God. This dangerous pattern can lead a priest to feel the need to escape and leave the priestly ministry altogether.

Many theologians in the last several decades have pointed to communion with Christ as the antidote to the disease of functionalism in the priesthood. Blessed Columba Marmion provided a helpful "definition" of communion with Christ in describing such communion as a tangible "contact" with God. This contact with God is something perceptible and is meant to be lived in a continual way throughout the priest's ministry. The way to living in continual contact with God is through prayer—prayer as an ongoing conversation with God as a child to its Father.

The Second Vatican Council emphasized how the objective union with Christ that is received through the Sacrament of Holy Orders needs to be subjectively appropriated by the priest. Simply put, the priest needs consciously to choose communion with Christ as the most important reality of his life. The Council teaches that this communion with Christ is a communion with Christ's own pastoral charity.

St. John Paul II taught us that the priest's identity is not found in his activity, but only in relationship with—in communion with—Jesus Christ. John Paul II also built upon the teaching of Vatican II on the centrality of pastoral charity in the life of the priest—the priest is called, in communion with Christ, to lay down his life for the flock.

Pope Benedict XVI took us even deeper into a theological understanding of the word "communion." In particular, Benedict taught us that communion means fellowship with Christ, participation in Him, and being joined intimately with Him. This communion involves the surrender of a person's will to God's will. Benedict made it absolutely clear that communion with Christ must be the very center of a priest's life, and that this communion comes about through daily prayer—prayer that includes a substantial degree of silence.

Finally, we saw how St. John Mary Vianney is a living image of what communion with Christ "looks like." The fact that Vianney was an extremely active diocesan priest, yet one who lived in a continual communion with Christ, gives much hope to diocesan priests today that such communion with

Christ is possible—indeed, absolutely essential—in a life of very active ministry.

If one is convinced of the fact that communion with Christ is the antidote to the disease of functionalism in the priesthood, two questions might be raised by a priest eager to live in communion with Christ. First, "If I were to 'check my pulse,' how would I *know* whether or not I am suffering from the disease of functionalism or living in communion with Christ?" Second, "How do I *remain* in communion with Christ?"

To arrive at an accurate answer to the first question, the priest really needs to explore this question with his own spiritual director. However, some general observations can be made based on the content of this book. As the priest "checks his pulse" and discovers that he is interiorly empty and is continually seeking to fill that emptiness with more and more activity, with the affirmation of the people he serves, with an excessive preoccupation about what he will do on his day off or when his next vacation will be, then he may very well be suffering from the disease of functionalism. He may find himself listening to or believing certain inner lies, such as: "I have to *do more* in order to feel that my life has meaning"; "I need to build something"; "I am important because I'm asked to speak at major events"; "I cannot afford to fail at anything"; "my next talk or homily needs to be better than the last one"; "I have no time to pray because there is too much to do," and so on.

A priest living in functionalism may find that he is more "driven" than "led." In other words, he is driven by his ego (or by the Enemy) rather than led by the Holy Spirit. His sense of being driven has a lot to do with building up, or at least sustaining, his own self-image. Much of this has do with people-pleasing and his need to gain the approval and affirmation of others. He is living on a horizontal, rather than a vertical, level.

Finally, a priest living in functionalism may notice in his heart the elements of "spiritual desolation" described by St. Ignatius of Loyola: "darkness of soul, disturbance in it, movement to low and earthly things, disquiet from various agitations and temptations, moving to lack of confidence, without hope, without love, finding oneself totally slothful, tepid, sad and, as if separated from one's Creator and Lord."[1]

In contrast, a priest will know that he is in communion with Christ if he has continually chosen to place Christ at the very center of his life. This priest may occasionally still experience an inner emptiness, but rather than fill this emptiness with more activity or with harmful behaviors, he turns to Jesus and cries out with Jesus to the Father, asking to be filled with Divine grace, mercy, and love. A priest in communion with Christ will often experience in his heart a tangible closeness to the Lord, not only in concrete times of prayer but throughout his daily life and ministry. Even when this tangible sense of closeness is not there, such a priest will choose in faith to live according to the truth that the Lord is, indeed, near and has not abandoned him. He will allow any sense of the Lord's absence to propel him to a greater hunger for God. Such seeking of the Lord is, in itself, a movement of communion with Christ.

A priest in communion with Christ is likely to have a heartfelt awareness of what St. Ignatius of Loyola means by "spiritual consolation," namely:

. . . the soul comes to be inflamed with love of its Creator and Lord, and, consequently . . . it can love no created thing on the face of the earth in itself, but only in the Creator of them all. . . . when it sheds tears that move to love of its Lord . . . [or experiences an] increase of hope, faith, and charity, and all interior joy that calls and attracts to heavenly things and to the salvation of one's soul, quieting it and giving it peace in its Creator and Lord.[2]

It should be noted that this definition of spiritual consolation is rather broad—it is not limited only to a feeling of God's presence, but also includes an increase of faith, hope, and charity.

It is important to mention that while there is value in "checking one's pulse" in order to know whether one is living in functionalism or in communion with Christ, it can, nonetheless, be harmful to be overly attached to the need to keep asking this question insofar as such self-evaluation can itself lead to isolation from the Lord rather than communion with Him. Communion with Christ involves a certain degree of self-forgetfulness. A patient who suffers from a physical illness can make his condition even worse by constantly checking his temperature. It would be better to simply seek out a doctor's assistance and then "let go" and trust that he will be taken care of. In the same way, a priest suffering from the disease of functionalism should seek out the Divine Physician, with the help of his spiritual director, and place himself securely in the Lord's hands. The simple movement of placing oneself in the Lord's hands may even be all that is necessary to move away from the condition of functionalism and back into communion with Christ.

To the second question of, "How do I remain in communion with Christ?" one need only look to all that has been said by saints and theologians down the centuries. A priest who desires to remain in communion with Christ should seek to incorporate in his life the following elements: a daily holy hour of personal prayer, the faithful praying of the Liturgy of the Hours, the daily celebration of Mass, the daily reading of Sacred Scripture, monthly spiritual direction in which the priest shares his struggles very honestly,[3] the daily examen prayer,[4] living in communion with one's bishop and brother priests, and the nourishing of silence and solitude in one's life—perhaps with the help of a monthly desert day of prayer.[5]

However, it is even possible for the above spiritual practices to become another form of functionalism. In other words, these practices could be another form of "doing"—they could be empty activities that are done on one's own in order to provide a sense of accomplishment. The priest could go to his spiritual director and say, "I've been very faithful to my holy hour this month," but when the director asks him to say more about how he is encountering the Lord within his prayer or within his life in general, the priest may not have much to say. As the *Catechism of the Catholic Church* puts it, "If our heart is far from God, the words of prayer are in vain."[6]

What is so essential, then, to remaining in communion with Christ is the priest's interior disposition more so than his external practices. The most important interior disposition is the virtue of poverty of spirit. In the Gospel of Matthew, Jesus names poverty of spirit as the first of the Beatitudes: "Blessed are the poor in spirit, for theirs is the kingdom of heaven" (Mt 5:3). In speaking about Jesus' own poverty, Fr.

Johannes Baptist Metz said that "To become human means to become 'poor,' to have nothing that one might brag about before God. To become human means to have no support and no power, save the enthusiasm and commitment of one's own heart."[7] The Evil One despises such poverty of spirit, and will constantly seek to dislodge it when he sees it: "Satan wants to make Jesus strong, for what the devil really fears is the powerlessness of God in the humanity Christ has assumed."[8] It is the self-emptying of Christ that leads to our salvation, and so, "Satan fears the trojan horse of an open human heart that will remain true to its native poverty, suffer the misery and abandonment that is humanity's, and thus save humankind."[9] Thus, if the priest is to remain in communion with Christ, and participate in Christ's saving mission, he must be willing to share in Jesus' own vulnerability and poverty of spirit.

To facilitate the reception of the virtue of poverty of spirit, it would be helpful to meditate upon these words from Fr. Tadeusz Dajczer, in his book *The Gift of Faith*: "Perceive yourself as a small grain of sand, as St. Thérèse spoke of herself—a small 'nothing,' who should not be cared for, or troubled with, or worried about too much. 'Pray,' wrote the saint, 'that the grain of sand become an ATOM seen only by the eyes of Jesus!'"[10] When one is as little as a grain of sand, or even as tiny as an atom, he will surely recognize his absolute dependence on God.

An important aspect of poverty of spirit is to have a healthy sense of humor. As Dajczer puts it, "Christian humor is a remedy that dethrones the idol of self."[11] He further asserts, "there is something that makes it impossible for God's mercy to be poured out, and something that God detests in you—it is your unwavering, absolute seriousness; it is your belief that you are someone important. Seeing this, it as though God makes a gesture of spreading out His hands in helplessness."[12] Dajczer says that "God finds your feeling of importance funny and absurd,"[13] and so we should try to laugh at ourselves. We grow in poverty of spirit as we realize and live the truth that the only one who should be taken seriously is God.[14]

Living in poverty of spirit, the priest in humility will be led to constantly seek only the Father's will in all things. One of the greatest resources for coming to know God's will is St. Ignatius of Loyola's *Rules for the Discernment of Spirits*. St. Ignatius teaches us the importance of the threefold dynamic of becoming aware of one's interior movements, understanding them, and taking action—accepting what comes from God and rejecting what is not of God.[15] This process will help the priest to stay very close to Christ.

What will also help the priest to remain in communion with Christ and live according to the Father's will is the discovery of his own personal vocation. Fr. Herbert Alphonso uses the term "personal vocation" to mean one's "truest and deepest self;" one's "God-given uniqueness;" in other words, one's unique identity in Christ.[16] Alphonso emphasizes that one's "personal vocation is *not* on the level of doing or of function but of *being*."[17] When a priest has this deep sense of who he is on the level of being, then what the priest *does* will easily flow from who he *is*: ". . . the personal vocation, once discerned, becomes *the criterion of discernment* for every decision in life, even for the daily details of decision making. For my personal vocation is for me 'God's will' in the deepest theological meaning of this . . . phrase."[18]

These necessary interior dispositions for remaining in communion with Christ can be summed up in this way: the priest's heart must be so firmly set on the Lord that God is absolutely first in the priest's life. What matters most is that the priest *desires* God and wants to live for Him alone. Here, the priest can take as his model the Blessed Virgin Mary, Mother of Priests. Mary's heart is so set on God that her entire being proclaims the Lord's greatness.[19] Our Blessed Mother is very eager to help her priest sons grow in communion with Christ. As we turn to Mary and grow in filial relationship with our Mother, our communion with the Blessed Trinity will deepen exponentially. As St. Louis Marie de Montfort puts it, "When Mary has taken root in a soul she produces in it wonders of grace which only she can produce; for she alone is the fruitful virgin who never had and never will have her equal in purity and fruitfulness."[20]

When priests really begin to respond to Christ's own desire for intimate and unceasing communion, the priesthood will be completely transformed: functionalism will be dispelled and the hearts of priests will be set on fire with love for God and His people. As the hearts of priests are awakened and enlivened, the lay faithful cannot help but catch this fire. As the lay faithful are drawn into communion with Christ themselves, the love of Christ will impel them to go out and "renew the face of the earth" (Ps 104:30).[21]

NOTES

1. Timothy Gallagher, *The Discernment of Spirits*, 8. Week 1, Rule 4.

2. Ibid., 7. Week 1, Rule 3.

3. Here, the priest might want to note the "Golden Rule" of spiritual direction: always tell your spiritual director whatever you most do NOT want to tell him! This is because the Enemy likes to "remain secret and not be revealed" (*Discernment of Spirits*, Week 1, Rule 13). However, bringing the truth to light sets us free as it opens us to receive Divine Love wherever we feel most unlovable.

4. For an excellent resource on this important spiritual practice, see Timothy M. Gallagher, *The Examen Prayer: Ignatian Wisdom for Our Lives Today* (New York: The Crossroad Publishing Company, 2005).

5. See Catherine de Hueck Doherty's *Poustinia: Encountering God in Silence, Solitude and Prayer* for an in-depth approach to a spirituality of the "desert." St. John Paul II also provides encouraging words about solitude: "It should be added that a certain type of solitude is a necessary element in ongoing formation. Jesus often went off alone to pray (cf. Mt. 14:23). The ability to handle a healthy solitude is indispensable for caring for one's interior life. Here we are speaking of a solitude filled with the presence of the Lord who puts us in contact with the Father, in light of the Spirit. In this regard, concern for silence and looking for places and times of 'desert' are necessary for the priest's permanent formation, whether in the intellectual, spiritual, or pastoral areas. In this regard too, it can be said that those unable to have a positive experience of their own solitude are incapable of genuine and fraternal fellowship." John Paul II, *Pastores Dabo Vobis* (1992), sec. 74.

6. *Catechism of the Catholic Church* (Washington, DC: USCCB Publishing, 2000), sec. 2562.

7. Johannes Baptist Metz, *Poverty of Spirit*, trans. John Drury (New York: Paulist Press, 1968, 1998).

8. Ibid.

9. Ibid., 10-11.

10. Tadeusz Dajczer, *The Gift of Faith*, 3rd ed. (Fort Collins, CO: In the Arms of Mary Foundation, 2012), 101.

11. Ibid.

12. Ibid., 97.

13. Ibid.

14. Ibid., 105.

15. Gallagher, *The Discernment of Spirits*, 16-17.

16. Herbert Alphonso, *Discovering Your Personal Vocation: The Search for Meaning through the Spiritual Exercises* (New York: Paulist Press, 2001), 2.

17.   Ibid., 28. Alphonso actually sums up the whole problem of functionalism here: "Again, it should be abundantly clear that the personal vocation is *not* on the level of doing or of function, but on the level of *being*. It is tragic—even literally so—that so many people interpret 'vocation' in terms of mere function or mere doing. Now, the level of function or of doing is bound to enter into crisis some day—that is of the very nature of function or of doing. If then, while in crisis, I have no resources of 'being' to fall back upon because my entire understanding of 'vocation' is resolved in terms of sheer function and mere doing, I shall be in total *crisis*. This is unfortunately the not infrequent, tragic story of quite a few lives. But if in such a crisis I can fall back on my resources of 'being'—so uniquely gifted to me in my personal vocation—I need have no fear; I can tide over that crisis, indeed integrate it, thanks to the very personal meaning on the level of being I can find in that very crisis. For all doing flows from being."

18.   Ibid., 43.

19.   See Luke 1:46-55.

20.   "True Devotion to Mary," *God Alone: The Collected Writings of St. Louis Marie de Montfort,* no. 35 (Bay Shore, NY: Montfort Publications, 1987), 299.

21.   See 2 Corinthians 5:14.

Epilogue
Father Ron Revisited

As Father Ron sits down to pray in his rectory chapel, his thoughts go toward all his achievements and accomplishments. He notices that despite these achievements, he still feels an emptiness inside. He recognizes a feeling of loneliness as well. But before he has a chance to really address these feelings, his mind starts racing about tonight's youth minister conference. He begins to panic. He is suddenly overwhelmed with a fear of failure. What if he "bombs" this talk? What will people think of him then?

Feeling a sense of desperation, he *turns to the Lord* and pours out his heart to Him. He gives voice to his fear of failure. He tells the Lord about the huge pressure he feels to "perform" well tonight. He sheds some tears as he names the loneliness and emptiness he feels. As he releases all his thoughts and emotions, he begins to feel some relief. It seems like God is really listening to him and is with him. There is peace and a sense of calm. A memory comes to him from his eight-day retreat when he was in the seminary. He had received an invitation from Jesus on that retreat to simply rest within His Sacred Heart. He feels the Lord inviting him again into this same place.

As he responds to this invitation, the words of Scripture flood into him, "Come to me, all you who labor and are burdened, and I will give you rest" (Mt. 11:28). These words fill Fr. Ron with great joy. Something is lifted from him. He feels lighter. There is a sense of the Father embracing him. He feels like the Father is saying to him, "You are my son, and I love you. I don't love you simply because of your achievements but because of who you are. Receive my love."

The feelings of loneliness and emptiness have disappeared. He knows now that he is not alone. He recognizes that he has been trying to earn love by way of his accomplishments, but the Father simply loves him as he is. This awareness leaves him free simply to live under the Father's gaze, within the heart of Jesus. He is being invited to live in deep communion with the Trinity.

As he rests there with the Trinity, Fr. Ron receives a further gift: he knows exactly what the Father wants him to speak about tonight. It is a simple message that comes to him with great ease, without needing to labor so much over it. And more importantly, he realizes that what matters even more than the content of his talk is that Jesus wants him to rest in His heart even while he is speaking. Filled with gratitude, Fr. Ron voices a prayer of surrender, asking for the grace to live always in intimate and unceasing union with God.

CPSIA information can be obtained
at www.ICGtesting.com
Printed in the USA
FSHW022118250419

9 780998 116426